David Steel's
Border Country

David Steel's
Border Country

David and Judy Steel

WITH PHOTOGRAPHS BY

Charlie Waite

WEIDENFELD AND NICOLSON

LONDON

For Graeme, Catriona, Rory and Billy, who – unlike us – all enjoyed a Border childhood.

AUTHOR'S ACKNOWLEDGMENT

I would like to thank all the people throughout the Borders, too numerous to mention, who have given help and encouragement in the preparation of this book. The following, however, have been of especial assistance in supplying and checking information: Brian Holton of the Ettrick and Lauderdale Museums Service, Archie Purves of the Hawick Knitwear Manufacturers Association, ex-standard-bearer David Mitchell, Mrs Ann Goodburn of Peebles and Denbeigh Kirkpatrick of Denholm.

I would also like to thank Lord Tweedsmuir for permission to reprint the extract from John Buchan's essay 'Angling in Still Waters', which appears on page 37.

This book has been a joint project, but the lion's share of the research and writing has been done by Judy, and I know that without her it would have remained – as it had been for many busy years – no more than a pleasant idea.

David Steel, Ettrick Bridge, 1985

Charlie Waite would like to thank Bill and Myra Row of the Gordon Arms, and his daughter Ella for her company.

FRONTISPIECE *The meeting of two romantic rivers – the Tweed and the Ettrick – at Lindean, between Selkirk and Galashiels.*

HALF TITLE *The rugged landscape of the hills which border Ettrick Forest and Tweeddale, seen from the single track road that wends its way between the Megget and Talla reservoirs.*

ISBN 0 297 78582 6

First published in Great Britain in 1985 by
George Weidenfeld and Nicolson Limited, 91 Clapham High Street, London SW4 7TA

Designed by Simon Bell

Typeset by Keyspools Ltd, Golborne, Lancs
Colour separations by Newsele Litho Ltd
Printed in Italy by LEGO, Vicenza

CONTENTS

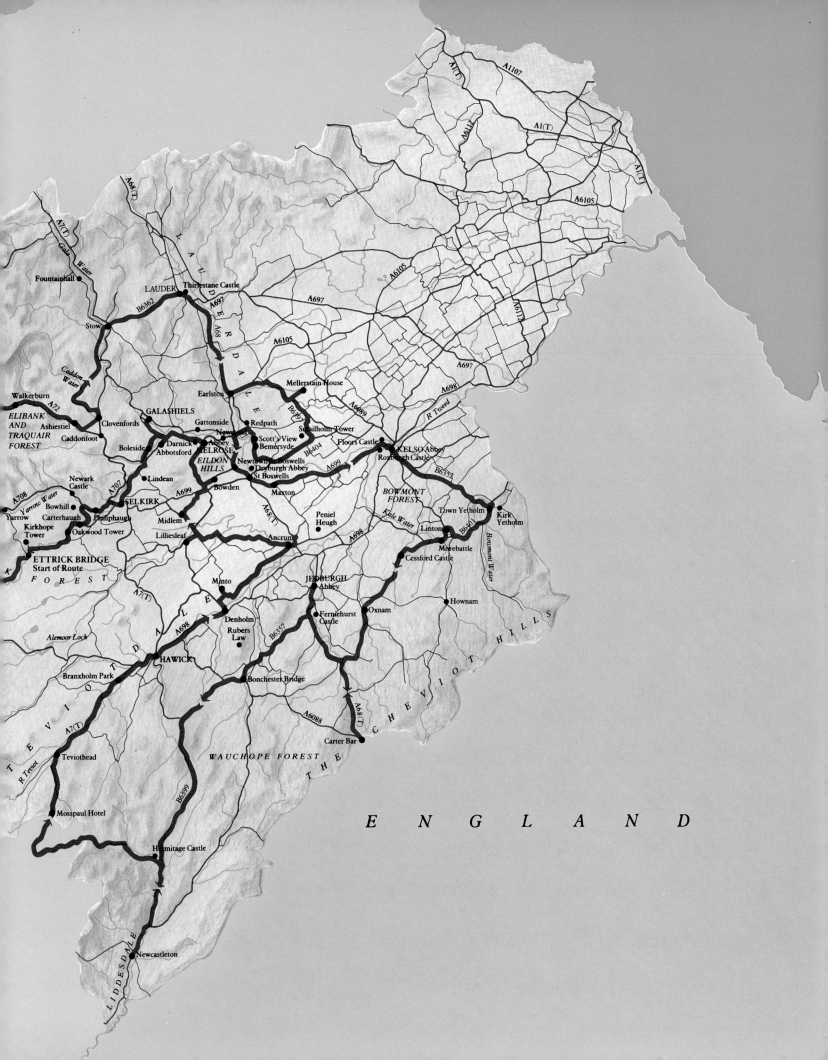

INTRODUCTION

There is a nineteenth-century poem by Lady John Scott which sums up the mood in which we came to the Borders over twenty years ago, though I did not know it then:

> When we first rade down Ettrick,
> Our bridles were ringing, our hearts were dancing,
> The waters were singing, the sun was glancing
> An' blithely our voices rang out thegither,
> As we brushed the dew frae the blooming heather,
>   When we first rade down Ettrick.

To be honest, it wasn't just the poetry of the Borders about which I was so woefully ignorant. I had to discover everything from scratch – all I really knew about were the post-war election figures.

If that makes it sound as though I was rushing hot-foot, carpetbag in hand, towards the best set of political statistics in Scotland, I should explain how it was that I came as Liberal candidate to the then constituency of Roxburgh, Selkirk and Peebles. Twenty-five years old, not long married, not long graduated, I was working in a junior position for the Party in Scotland, and had been adopted as a candidate for an interesting seat in Edinburgh. In the heady post-Orpington days of the 1960s the Liberals' prospects didn't, in my eyes, look as hopeless as modern interpreters describe; and anyway I am a perpetual optimist.

Our planned schedule for the early years of our married life went like this: I would fight the 1964 election, do reasonably well but not, I anticipated, well enough to win. Establish myself as the challenger; that was more like it. Then my wife Judy and I would go off for a couple of years to Kenya where I had spent the happiest part of my boyhood, get that out of my system, and return in time to work a constituency for the next election.

It was the Border Liberals who changed all that, and changed my life. The candidate for Roxburgh, Selkirk and Peebles had resigned. The old Roxburgh and Selkirk seat had been held by a Liberal in the 1950s, and we had always at least held second place there. They had very definite ideas about who they did and didn't want as a candidate, and actually turned down Russell Johnston on the grounds that he wore a kilt: 'And a kilt is Highland dress and would not go down at all in the Borders. Not at all.'

OPPOSITE *A remote sheep farm in the Liddesdale hills, where rough winter conditions have produced hardy breeds of both man and beast.*

9

The dawn of history in the Borders is uncharted. This stone, in the Yarrow valley, marks the grave of 'two sons of Liberalis'.

They decided that they wanted me. I had not asked them to consider me; I was quite happy where I was. Besides, I didn't know a thing about the area, and indeed was very much a city product. My earlier doubts about the whole reality of fighting a rural seat had disappeared after my involvement in two such by-elections had convinced me that the ability to understand rural issues did not require a country boyhood or a degree in agriculture. But the Borders was very different from the rest of Scotland – very independent and very jealous of its own traditions.

My work, though it took me around Scotland, was based in Edinburgh, and Judy worked there. In the Edinburgh constituency we did a lot of the work together; how feasible would this be when it came to nursing a seat which stretched from just outside the city right down to the English border – a vast area of scattered communities. But Judy was enthusiastic not primarily because of the political advantages but because the area appealed to her romantic streak. She knew a few Border ballads and Wordworth's Yarrow poems, she knew her

Scottish history, and unlike me she had a tenuous link with the area. She had been at school for a year, between the tender ages of five and six, in a grand Victorian mansion called Glenmayne just outside Galashiels.

Tentatively we met four representatives of the local party in the North British Hotel in Edinburgh. They were a formidable quartet in their fifties and sixties. One was Andrew Haddon, a solicitor and farmer from Hawick whose scholarliness and depth and breadth of knowledge is constantly displayed in the correspondence columns of the *Scotsman* newspaper. In everyday matters he is sometimes a trifle absent-minded. 'My dear,' he asked his wife one day, 'have you seen the car? I don't seem to have seen it for about three days.' It transpired that he had been motoring towards Hawick, where his office was situated, when he saw one of his cattle straying on a grass verge. He stopped the car, got out, put the beast in its field and then, having boarded an approaching bus, forgot he had started the journey in his car and continued to use the bus service for the next three days. His knowledge of the history of the Borders and its elections are total, and immensely detailed.

Will Stewart wasn't a native Borderer, but had lived there for many years and owned a mill at Galashiels producing high-quality tweeds and mohair. He had worked for Jo Grimond's campaigns in Orkney, and for the Liberal victory in the Borders in 1950. So he was, in those days, something of a rarity – a Party worker whose candidates had achieved electoral success. Winning elections was a reality to him, and indeed to all those who had been active in politics in the Borders for a little more than a decade. Will, who was then in his sixties, was as passionately romantic about Scotland as a honeymooning tourist or a third generation emigrant, and continued to be throughout his life. He had one of the most giving natures I ever encountered, and when he died our children mourned him too.

The remaining members of the quartet were both farmers: Jack Bryce had a hill farm in that most remote of valleys, the Kale Water, which stretches south of Kelso through the tiny village of Hownam and peters out among the Cheviot Hills on the English border; Willie Pate became the last Provost of Galashiels before the whole system of local government in Scotland was radically reorganized in 1974, eroding so many of the old traditions. He later quarrelled with the Liberal Association – it was a personal feud rather than a political one – and joined the Scottish Nationalists. He was the kind of Scot who appears so often in fiction that one could be lulled into thinking he could not possibly exist in real life. Utterly convinced of his own rightness in every issue, his substantial figure and dogmatic sureness made him an attractive civic leader in the old burgh tradition. He was a great opponent of kilt-wearing candidates, ipso facto, whatever their other qualities might be, and of Roman Catholics. Of all Liberal policies, the one he espoused most enthusiastically was that of proportional representation. On that subject he could hold forth for hours, and frequently did so as a supporting speaker at elections.

These then were the ambassadors sent to woo me from a fairly comfortable

A stretch of the Tweed near St Boswells, running unusually low after a long, hot summer.

RIGHT *The lands of Tushielaw in the Ettrick valley, once the home of the notorious sixteenth-century freebooter Adam Scott.*

12

and predictable niche. They were wily enough to appeal less to my sense of ambition – that would have been too crude – than to my sense of duty. No doubt they calculated that a marked development of that attribute was part of any manse upbringing. Their argument was that, unless they got the standard-bearer they wanted – in other words, me – they would probably not fight the seat. Elections in the Borders were gritty, rumbustuous events, and they needed to feel really confident in their choice. They wouldn't go ahead otherwise. It was an irresistible bargaining point, and the seat was clearly winnable – though probably not on the first occasion. The more I listened the more I became convinced I had to move.

Events took their course. In January 1964 I became the new prospective candidate for Roxburgh, Selkirk and Peebles. Three months later Judy and I took our second gamble: we gave up the lease of our cottage on the outskirts of Edinburgh and moved into a large farmhouse rented to us by the Laird of Gala, Christopher Scott, who became a close friend. I often think how different life might have been had we been successful in buying a house in Edinburgh during the previous eighteen months of our marriage – we would surely have been less cavalier about selling up than we were about giving up a rented cottage.

So we moved here. And the summer of 1964 stretched ahead, in which I was to explore and discover the countryside, the towns and customs, the mills and the farms and the now placid valleys. I began my courtship of the Border electorate before the election scheduled for that autumn. And if courtship is the right phrase, and if I fell in love with my future constituency, uncovering every day more surprises and delights, then I would hope that my subsequent relationship has been not so much a love affair as a marriage – rich, lasting, and a constant source of mutual support.

But that was a contract forged in the heat of elections; and before I embark with you on a journey round the delights of what is not only one of the most beautiful but also one of the most individual areas of the country, I should tell you more about it in general terms and about my own relationship with it in particular.

I was right in supposing that it would take me more than one attempt to win Roxburgh, Selkirk and Peebles. But it took a shorter time than I had imagined. In the general election of 1964 I came within two thousand votes of victory; and, six weeks later, the sitting member died. The by-election, held in 1965, caused great excitement, and I was returned to Parliament with four and a half thousand more votes than my Tory opponent, a few days before my twenty-seventh birthday.

Until the boundaries were redrawn in 1983 I continued to represent the three counties of Roxburgh, Selkirk and Peebles, with majorities ranging from three to five figures, and it is these counties, plus the territory carved out from Berwickshire and Midlothian to form the new constituency of Tweeddale, Ettrick and Lauderdale, that I will explore in this book.

The area ranges from the village of Carlops in Peeblesshire (now Tweeddale), just outside Edinburgh in the north, to Newcastleton in the south, whence many people commute to Carlisle. It spreads from Broughton and Skirling in the west, whose nearest city is Glasgow, to Kelso in the east, not far from the town of Berwick. Through it flows the River Tweed and its many tributaries: the Teviot, Jed, Ettrick, Yarrow, Gala and Leithen. The old parliamentary seat – the only one covering three counties – extended to seventeen hundred square miles. There were eight burghs – towns which, under the old system of local government, had their own town councils – ranging in size from Hawick with an electorate of about sixteen thousand to Innerleithen with about three thousand. In 1983, three of these – Hawick, Kelso and Jedburgh – became part of the new Roxburgh and Berwick constituency, while Lauder joined the remainder to form Tweeddale, Ettrick and Lauderdale; a network of villages covers the countryside between.

The economy of the Borders depends largely on agriculture and the woollen textile and knitwear industries, now using mainly imported rather than local wool. Recently, as employment prospects in the textile industry have declined, electronics and micro-circuit manufacturing companies have moved into the area, as well as a proliferation of small businesses involved in light industry. Tourism also accounts for a growing sector of the economy as more and more people discover the delights of the Border countryside, so often bypassed in the race northwards to the Scottish capital and the Highlands.

The landscape here is one of gently rolling hills of great natural beauty, and the area is rich not only with scenic attractions but also with great houses and an amazing store of literary, legendary and historic associations.

OPPOSITE *A burn in the higher reaches of Ettrick Forest.*

This was the front line of the centuries-old struggle beteeen two warring nations, one comparatively rich and aggressive, the other poor and struggling to maintain her independence. It was the source of a great heritage of ballads, telling stories of feats of valour, of love and betrayal, and of supernatural forces. And it was the home and inspiration of such great literary figures as Sir Walter Scott, James Hogg, John Buchan and Andrew Lang.

I have chosen to present this portrait of the Borders – of some of its most influential figures and families, its battles, traditions, industries and landmarks – in the form of a circular tour of the region, starting and finishing at my home in Ettrick Bridge. It cannot be comprehensive, but I hope no reader will be left in any doubt as to why I return week after week to this exceptionally beautiful place.

ONE

ETTRICK AND YARROW

We came to live in Ettrick Bridge by chance. On paper it seemed too remote to be convenient for the rest of the constituency, but once we had seen the house we recognized it as our ideal. In 1966, throwing caution to the winds, we bought it smack in the middle of the first general election at which I was seeking re-election, and thereafter we managed to persuade ourselves that Ettrick was in fact the centre point of my political area. The village, of less than a hundred inhabitants, has changed little in physical terms since the beginning of the century, and it turned out to be an idyllic place to bring up a young family – which began to arrive after our move – for it provided a freedom that is rare in the experience of children in Britain today. James Hogg's classic evocation of an unsullied boyhood is still pertinent:

> Where the pools are bright and deep,
> Where the grey trout lies asleep,
> Up the river and o'er the lea,
> That's the way for Billy and me.

Through this natural paradise runs the Ettrick Water. J.B. Selkirk, a popular poet of the early part of this century, lovingly traces the course of the river from its source to its confluence with the Tweed in 'Epistle to Tammas', an imaginary letter from a Border emigré to a friend in Ettrick. This is how he describes the river at Ettrick Bridge:

> And then is there a bonnier bit
> On ony water, head to fit,
> Where, tumblin' doon the rugged streams,
> The lashing water froths and creams,
> Till o'er the salmon-loup it spins
> 'Tween green Helmburn and Kirkhope Linns,
> Where Ettrick rins?

Up the river from the village is the manse pool, hemmed in between tumbling falls at either end, while to right and left rise the rocky cliffs known as the Linns, whose formation gives the area special geological and scientific interest. In summer its dark surface is never rippled except by the rings of a rising trout. Downstream the Ettrick falls in a fan-shaped cascade to the Glebe pool, and on

OPPOSITE *The Ettrick Water, as it tumbles in spate over rocks high up in the hills.*

the adjoining rocky outcrop, bog-myrtle, marsh marigold, and tiny, pallid violets grow. In the lower cliffs dogroses, hawthorn and rowan saplings insinuate their roots into crevices, while the summits are crowned with birch, pine, holly and elm.

To start this tour of the Borders, take the road up the valley, away from the village and from the six-mile-distant town of Selkirk. As the road unfolds along Ettrick, keeping the river as its companion all the way, almost every place-name – Dodhead, Deloraine, Gilmanscleuch, Tushielaw, Rankleburn – reverberates with the echoes of legend and poetry. Scarcely half a mile from the village is the first tangible reminder of the past: Kirkhope Tower, a peel tower standing in a commanding position on the hillside; it was the property of one of the most famous of all the Border reivers.

Peel towers and reivers are an integral part of Border history, scenery and legend, and they require some explanation. Throughout the troubled Middle Ages people customarily took refuge together when threatened with a raid.

18

Such raids were part of incessant Border warfare as Scotland struggled to maintain her identity and independence in the face of relentless aggression from England. The need for protection from enemy attack produced a series of fortified buildings, of which the most elementary was the 'pele-house'. Its name may derive from *pyle*, meaning a pile of stones, although there are other explanations. Some of the 'pele-houses' were so rudimentary that they were not even used for living in: traces of fireplaces incorporated into the structure identify those that were inhabited. The proliferation of peel towers (as they came to be called) throughout the Borders, many of which are still standing and a few of them still habitable, was the result of systematic planning. It was laid down that all lairds in ownership of a certain acreage of land were required to construct such a building in order to establish a coherent line of defence, along which beacons were lit in times of danger.

The reiver was a product of his geographical location, and, like so much else in the Borders, he has no counterpart elsewhere in Scotland, let alone Britain. In this eternal battleground between two nations, people lived under a constant threat of strife. And men adapted to this by forming their own rules of conduct. The reivers were freebooters, or mosstroopers. They did not form a criminal class but came from all walks of life, went about their ordinary business, whatever that might be, and reived as well – riding to and fro in the rolling hills, fighting, burning, taking booty, and above all, cattle. They were echoing what the armies of Scotland and England had done to them and theirs on a grand scale over the centuries. They were highly skilled guerilla soldiers whose ingenuity, tactics and local knowledge might be envied by many a liberation movement today.

But they were not liberators. They roamed out to their neighbours' lands – and their neighbours might well be on the same side of the border – and returned with their takings, for a living, not for a political purpose. The historian and poet Satchells summed them up thus:

> I would have none think that I call them thieves.
> The freebooter ventures both life and limb
> Good wife, and bairn, and efery other thing;
> He must do so, or else starve and die,
> For all his livelihood comes of the enemy.

And Bishop Leslie's description of them at around the same time depicts them as anything but bloodthirsty: 'The shedding of blood they greatly abhor. They make war with all possible diligence that they shed not their blood who are contrary to them.' And he sums up neatly the attitude of the sixteenth-century Borderer to property: he is 'persuaded that all the goods of all men in time of necessity are by the law of nature common'.

The Archbishop of Glasgow in the mid-sixteenth century (the heyday of the Border reivers) was less charitable. His 'Great Cursing' is hard to match for pure invective:

20

I curse thair heid and all the haris of thair heid; I curse thair face, thair ene, thair mouth, thair neise, thair toung, thair teith, thair crag, thair schulderrs, thair breist, thair hert, thair stomak, thair bak, thair wame, thair armes, thair leggis, thair handis, thair feit, and everilk part of thair body, frae the top of thair heid to the soill of thair feit, befoir and behind, within and without . . . I curse thaim ganand [going] and I curse thaim rydand (riding); I curse thaim standand and I curse them sittand; I curse thaim etand, and I curse thaim drinkand; I curse them walkand, and I curse them sleepand; I curse thaim rysand and I curse thaim lyand; I curse thaim at hame, I curse thaim frae hame; I curse thaim within the house, I curse thaim without the house; I curse thair wiffis, thair barnis, and thair servandis participand with them in thair deides . . .'

Has there, I wonder, ever been such comprehensive cursing?

Wat o'Harden, an ancestor and namesake of Sir Walter Scott, built Kirkhope Tower at the end of the sixteenth century. He was one of the most notable – or notorious, according to your point of view – of all the reivers. At his most rampant in the 1590s, his raids south brought back hundreds of head of cattle, not to mention horses and spoil. Nor, according to legend, was his live booty limited to quadrupeds. There are two versions of the tale that credits Wat o'Harden with having taken home from Northumberland an infant, snatched mistakenly by one of his men with a pile of hangings and silks. One version, commemorated in Will Ogilvie's fine ballad 'Whaup o' the Rede', describes the child's upbringing with Wat's own warlike son Will, his quarrel with his foster brother and father, his tracing of his natural mother and his eventual reconciliation with the Scotts. Another version is that the child was swept from 'Auld Wat's' arms when fording the Ettrick in spate on his return journey; and that the great reiver, struck with remorse, constructed the original bridge near where the present one now stands, incorporating his coat of arms.

Wat o'Harden took part in one of the most colourful and humanitarian of all the Border raids, when his overlord and namesake, Walter Scott of Buccleuch – 'The Bold Buccleuch' – set off with a party of hand-picked men to rescue another redoubtable reiver, William Armstrong. The action-packed ballad 'Kinmont Willie' describes the foray which, without loss of life, brought Armstrong back from imprisonment and certain death at Carlisle Castle. Less reputably, he joined forces with Francis, the last Earl of Bothwell, in his attempt to capture King James VI in 1592. Since reprisals against Auld Wat included the destruction of his castle at Harden, near Hawick, he may well have spent longer periods at Kirkhope thereafter.

Wat's family reflected some of the colourfulness of his own character. His beautiful wife, Mary of Dryhope, known as the Flower of Yarrow, reputedly served him a dish of spurs when the larder ran low, indicating that it was time her husband took to the saddle again in search of replenishment. Of their six sons, the eldest, Will, seems to have been the most like his father; but the story of his unconventional courtship belongs to a later chapter.

Not only did Ettrick breed bold raiding men and their supportive womenfolk; it also provided Scotland with one of her literary giants. James Hogg, the Ettrick Shepherd, was part of the movement that saw the flowering of a Scottish golden age of letters, and his birthplace a few miles up the valley, and his resting place in the shadowed graveyard at Ettrick Kirk, are worth a visit.

Hogg was born in 1770, into a family who had fallen on hard times. His ancestors had been substantial farmers, but his father's lack of success at farming ventures – a failing inherited by his son – had brought them down in the world. Hogg's formal schooling consisted of six months at the age of six, during which he learnt to read the Shorter Catechism and the Proverbs of Solomon. Thereafter, family finances required him to earn his own meagre keep as a herd laddie. But his education in the great oral traditions of the district was second to none, for his teacher was his mother, Margaret Laidlaw, who was renowned as the finest ballad-teller around. Ironically it was her fame, she believed, that brought that heritage to an end, for it was she whom Sir Walter Scott used as the source of much of his research on the ballads, and she foresaw the consequences: 'Mr Scott, there was never ane o' ma songs prentit till ye prentit them yersel', an' ye hae spoilt them athegither. They war made for singing an' no' for reading; and they're neither richt spelt not richt setten down.' Margaret Laidlaw's father was 'the far-famed Will o'Phaup, who for feats of frolic, strength and agility, had no equal in his day'. What an epitaph! He was the last person who actually claimed to have seen and conversed with the fairies, whose adventures form such a substantial part of his grandson's best works.

Hogg's great piece of fortune, as far as his intellectual and literary unfolding was concerned, came when he went as a shepherd to the farm of Mr Laidlaw of Blackhouse, in Yarrow. Here, he was enveloped in a household both widely read and intelligent. They were also encouraging when, in his twenties, Hogg began scribbling verses as he tended the sheep. Much to his own gratification, he became known as 'Jamie the Poeter', and when he eventually discovered the works of Robert Burns, he determined to be his successor.

But Hogg's poetry was really of a different genre. He lacked Burns' political commitment, and his ever-vulnerable romantic passions. He was at his best describing the countryside he knew so well, or in the realms of the supernatural. There, talent flies away in the face of genius, for only genius could have produced 'Kilmeny', as this extract from it illustrates:

> When many lang day had come and fled,
> When grief grew calm, and hope was dead,
> When mess for Kilmeny's soul had been sung,
> When the bedes-man had prayed, and bell had been rung;
> When the fringe was red on the westin hill,
> The wood was sere, the moon i' the wane,
> The reek o' the cot hung o'er the plain,
> Like a little wee cloud in the world its lane:
> When the ingle nook lowed wi' an eiry leme,
> Late, late in the gloamin Kilmeny came hame.

Shadowy Ettrick churchyard holds the graves of James Hogg and his family, and of the influential theologian Thomas Boston, who was parish minister here from 1707 to 1732.

LEFT *The Ettrick Shepherd gazes towards his beloved hills from his memorial at the head of St Mary's Loch.*

'. . . a silvery current flows
With uncontrolled meanderings;
Nor have these eyes, by greener hills
Been soothed, in all my wanderings.'
(Wordsworth : 'Yarrow Visited')

Nor was his genius confined to poetry. Among his many prose works, *Confessions of a Justified Sinner* must rank as the most profound, penetrating and mystical novel ever to come out of Scotland, dealing as it does with the recesses of the national psyche, with Calvinist dogma, and with haunting and unworldly forces beyond human explanation.

Although the 'Queen's Wake', of which 'Kilmeny' formed a part, caused a literary sensation, it was only in London that Hogg was fêted and lionized. He was never really accepted in fashionable Edinburgh society, and would not adapt his manners to suit the niceties of the capital, often appearing gruff or even boorish. At best, he was regarded as a loved eccentric; at worst, as a kind of court jester, a buffoon. But he sailed through life regardless, supremely and rightly confident of his own genius, and disdaining to compromise.

His relationship with Sir Walter Scott was stormy: it never had the flavour, which it should have had, of a meeting of literary equals; it seems always to have been one of patron and protégé. And the Shepherd's reaction was typical of

24

The old rough track leading to St Mary's Loch, over hills where forestry is encroaching on the traditional sheep pastures. A sign warns motorists that they attempt this route at their own risk.

such a relationship: he loved Scott, he respected him, and he resented him from time to time.

Leaving Ettrick for its twin valley, Yarrow, we do not leave the Ettrick Shepherd behind, for he spent much of his life beside that most ballad-haunted of rivers. We meet Yarrow not far from the old property of Altrive, where Hogg lived out the last years of his life contentedly with the young wife and family of his late middle age. A left turn at the Gordon Arms takes us towards dramatic St Mary's Loch and the smaller Loch o' the Lowes. On the isthmus straddling them stands Hogg's statue, near the old hostelry known as Tibbie Shiels' Inn. Tibbie was a resourceful woman, a contemporary of Hogg and Scott, who turned her hand to innkeeping when the death of her husband left her with a young family to support. Her warmth and hospitality, and down-to-earth good sense, became a byword, and the tiny cottage prospered as an inn, and still does. Some of the most memorable Burns suppers I have attended have taken place there, and when I hear anyone announce that they are 'away up to Tibbie's' it is

25

as if she still presides there herself. Nowadays the Southern Upland Way passes her door, a walker's route linking west coast to east along southern Scotland.

Yarrow today presents a pastoral, tranquil scene, as it did to Wordsworth on his visit there in 1814:

> Fair scenes for childhood's opening bloom,
> For sportive youth to play in,
> For manhood to enjoy his strength;
> And age to wear away in!

but it is stained with legends of ill-fated love, of blood-feuds, treachery and tragedy. 'The Border Widow's Lament', perhaps the most poignant of all the Border ballads, is traditionally believed to tell the story of the Cockburns of Henderland, near St Mary's Loch. During his campaign to pacify the unruly Borders, King James v allegedly hanged William Cockburn at his own gate, and the ballad is said to describe the feelings of his widow:

27

My love he built me a bonny bower,
An' clad it a' wi' lilye flower,
A brawer bower ye ne'er did see,
Than my true love he built for me.

There came a man, by middle day,
He spied his sport, and went away;
And brought the king that very night,
Who brake my bower, and slew my knight.

He slew my knight, to me sae dear;
He slew my knight, and poin'd his gear;
My servants all for life did flee
And left me in extremitie.

I sew'd his sheet, making my mane;
I watched the corpse, myself alane;
I watched his body, night and day;
No living creature came that way.

I took his body on my back,
And whiles I gaed, and whiles I sat;
I digged a grave, and laid him in,
And happed him wi' the sod sae green.

But think na ye my heart was sair
When I laid the mould on his yellow hair:
O think na ye my heart was wae,
When I turned about, awa' to gae?

Nae living man I'll love again
Since that my lovely knight is slain;
Wi' ae lock o' his yellow hair,
I'll chain my heart for evermair.

It is impossible to mention here all the ballads set in Yarrow. Some people believe that the author of many of them was the young man brought up as a son by Wat o' Harden and the Flower of Yarrow – a fanciful but pleasing idea.

The old church of St Mary's of the Lowes features in many of them, though all that is left of it now is a windswept, weatherbeaten churchyard, which every year sees the only tangible reminder of another troubled time in Scotland's history. In the seventeenth century the civil wars in which the foolish King Charles I embroiled his subjects were, north of the border, of religious and not of constitutional origin. His attempts to enforce episcopalianism on the unwilling Scots led to the first resistance to his sovereignty, and to the final defeat of his cause in Scotland at Philiphaugh, at the other end of the Yarrow valley. But the revenge exacted by his sons, Charles II and James VII, on the successors of those who had signed the National Covenant in defiance of their father, was extreme. Ministers were driven from their parishes and unwelcome

OPPOSITE *Church services are now held only once a month at Cappercleuch Church, built in the last century as a United Free Church.*

vicars imposed on congregations in their place. The result was that people took to the hills to hear the word of God preached, in accordance with their beliefs, in the open air. The conventicles were broken up by the military, and the adherents dreadfully persecuted and harassed. My own namesake and ancestor, the covenanting David Steel, was shot at his Lanarkshire home in front of his children and his stoical wife. Gathering up the fragments of his skull, she remarked that it was better to perish thus than to lose sight of the true faith. In St Mary's churchyard every July the troubles and sacrifices of those times are remembered in the open air 'Blanket Preaching' commemorating the days when people huddled under blankets to listen to the sermons of the outlawed ministers. *The Brownie of Bodseck* by the Ettrick Shepherd provides a vivid picture both of the terrors undergone by the Covenanters and of the wildness of the countryside in which they took refuge:

There is a range of high mountains bordering on Annandale, Ettrick Forest and Tweeddale, that are by many degrees the wildest, the most rugged, and inaccessible in the South of Scotland. They abound with precipitous rocks, caverns and waterfalls, besides interminable morasses, full of deep ruts, which are nevertheless often green and dry at the bottom, with perhaps a small rill tinkling along each of them. No superior hiding place can be conceived. With means of subsistence, thousands of men might remain there in safe concealment, with the connivance of a single shepherd. To that desolate and unfrequented region did the shattered remains of the routed fugitives from the field of Bothwell Bridge, as well as the broken and persecuted whigs from all the western districts, ultimately flee as to their last refuge . . .

It was a season of calamity and awful interest. From the midst of that inhospitable wilderness, from those dark morasses and unfrequented caverns, the prayers of the persecuted race rose nightly to the throne of the almighty. In the solemn gloom of the evening, after the last rays of day had disappeared, and again in the morning before the ruddy streaks began to paint the East, songs of praise were sung to that Being under whose fatherly chastisement they were patiently suffering. These hymns, always chanted with ardour and wild melody, and borne afar on the breezes at twilight, were often heard at a great distance, causing no little consternation to the remote dwellers of that mountain region. The heart of the shepherd grew chill, and his hairs stood on end, as he hastened home to alarm the cottage circle with a tale of horror. For, besides this solemn and unearthly music, he perceived lights moving about in wilds and in caverns where human thing had never resided, and where foot of man had never trod, and he deemed that legions of spiritual creatures had once more taken possession of his solitary dells.

It is this countryside through which we now pass.

TWO

UPPER TWEEDSMUIR

The old single-track road through Megget lies buried now beneath the tons of water in the new reservoir which serves the population of Edinburgh. Along with it lies the old village school (which still had six pupils when I first came to the Borders), a few farms which offered a hard living for their occupants, and the upper reaches of Ettrick Forest, that vast wild pleasure-ground of the Stuart kings. The modern road which now runs high along the hillside is scenic enough in the sunshine, with its carefully arranged viewpoints and picnic places, but in overcast or stormy weather it comes into its own, the sombre waters obliterating the history below it and the barren scree reaching to the mountaintops above.

After twists and turns, the road meets Talla, that doyen of reservoirs, which was built at the beginning of this century. At its foot stands the lovely parish church of Tweedsmuir, in whose churchyard lie the remains of the covenanting martyr John Hunter.

HERE LYES JOHN HUNTER
MARTYR WHO WAS CRUELY
MURDERED AT COREHEAD
BY COL : JAMES DOUGLAS AND
HIS PARTY FOR HIS ADHERENCE
TO THE WORD OF GOD AND
SCOTLAND'S COVENANTED
WORK OF REFORMATION
1685

Erected in the year 1726.

OPPOSITE The snow lingers on the hilltops above Megget until well into the spring.

It is a quiet resting place after a violent death. Around Tweedsmuir the countryside is gentle, wooded, undisturbed, denoting the quality of life of those who made its history. If in the past, the lower reaches of the Tweed ran blood-red, here at its source the river is peaceful and has seen less of drama and turbulence.

From Tweedsmuir, the main Moffat to Peebles road passes the Crook Inn, whose origins go back to 1604. In covenanting days the resourceful landlady of the time found an unusual and highly effective hiding place for a fugitive: she built him into her stack of peat. Later, the inn became a changing-post for the

33

A view down Talla burn to the great reservoir it helps to feed.

RIGHT *Talla Reservoir, completed at the beginning of this century, is one of three reservoirs in the region supplying the needs of Edinburgh.*

The hills between Tweeddale and Ettrick Forest, described by Hogg as 'rugged and inaccessible'.

LEFT *The skills which go into the building of dry stone dykes are in short supply nowadays, and any young man prepared to master the craft is assured of ready work.*

horses of the mail coaches, but seems to have fallen under bad management in the early nineteenth century: a traveller in 1807 described it as 'one of the coldest-looking, cheerless places of reception for travellers that we had ever chanced to behold'. Its fortunes must have improved, however, for forty years later the same traveller writes that it had, 'comparatively speaking, an inviting air of comfort about it'.

One of the Crook Inn's present attractions lies in its 1930s conversion. No planning authority would pass it today but, unlike the ugly additions which have spoiled Tibbie Shiels' Inn, the Crook Inn's extensions have a harmony and a period charm of their own. Curved metal-framed windows, bright brick fireplaces and sumptuously tiled lavatories have turned parts of the building into a 1930s time-capsule. And buried away in its heart is the original stone-flagged bar, a nugget worth searching for.

Although the Crook Inn has associations with Scott and Hogg, Tweedsmuir belongs – in a literary sense – to a more recent writer, John Buchan, who took his title of first Baron Tweedsmuir from this parish. Born in 1875, Buchan was one of those giant, multi-talented figures that Scotland casts on to the world stage so consistently. His fame as an author rests mainly on the timeless, worldwide appeal of his adventure stories, which have thrilled every generation since their publication: *The Thirty-Nine Steps*, *Huntingtower*, *Greenmantle*, *Prester John*, to mention but a few. But Buchan's success as an author was only one of his achievements, and the diversity of his activities – as writer, politician, soldier, scholar, churchman and, finally, as Governor-General of Canada – can be fully appreciated after a visit to the newly opened John Buchan Centre just south of the village of Broughton.

Like Scott, Buchan was born outside the Borders but was of Border lineage – though of less swashbuckling descent than Scott's from Wat o'Harden. Buchan's paternal grandfather was a lawyer in Peebles, where the firm of J. & W. Buchan still exists. His maternal grandfather's farm was in Broughton, and it was here that his parents met and married, in the church which now houses the excellent small museum celebrating his achievements. In this village the young Buchan spent many happy childhood holidays, as lasting in their influence as were Scott's with his aunt at Smailholm. 'Since ever I was a very little boy', he wrote in 1901, 'I have liked Broughton better than any place in the world.' And, like Hogg, Buchan learnt the tales and folklore of the Borders at the parental knee; his father, the Rev. John Buchan, was a renowned and gifted storyteller, and passed on the traditions that fired his son's prolific imagination.

Like so many others, Buchan discovered that the ultimate balm for frayed nerves, and the most complete form of relaxation, was to be found in fishing. It is good to learn, too, that this son of the manse was not averse, as a boy, to abandoning more legal forms of the sport for the excitement of poaching. There can be few boys brought up in the Border countryside who have not sampled this risky, heady delight. Buchan himself had a brush with the law as a result of a poaching adventure, and perhaps his descriptive powers in recounting similar incidents later in life were enhanced as a result. This extract from his wonderful essay 'Angling in Still Waters' brings out the joys of the more conventional approach to fishing; it also gives us a description of this part of Peeblesshire which cannot be matched.

The rich woods of Rachan lie directly below us, forming a strange contrast in their bright green dress to the dark sombre pines on the hillside, or the still darker moorland beyond. Another quarter of a mile brings us to the end of the heath, and we cross a stile and enter the woods. Here there is a very superabundance of animal life. Blackbirds and thrushes fly screaming over our heads, yellow hammers and redbreasts hop across the path, while a hen chaffinch, dressed like a little Puritan, flits past attended by the gay cavalier cock. The ground is richly carpeted with moss, varied here and there with great patches of blackberries with unripened green fruit. Large tufts of ladyfern adorn the roots, and, where the rock crops up, polypodies and hardferns. The stone here is whinstone, but deep in the wood a solitary vein of trap crops up, on which I have found that rare little fern, the forked spleenwort. The sunlight, after filtering through these leafy screens above our head, comes down grateful and pleasant; and we feel the mossy coolness which one can find only in such a wood. But the trees are growing scarcer, and we see the low stone dyke which marks the end of the wood. Beyond is a short belt of velvet turf, and then a silvery gleam which we know must be the Tweed. We quicken our steps, and high hopes arise in our hearts, for what angler ever could resist a certain feeling of nervous trepidation at the sight of his stream? There are such grand possibilities in it; such monstrous fish, maybe, hidden under these shining waters, which it may be his lot to capture. But here we must stay and put our tackle together, for on such a day the river must be approached with caution. We put on an extra fine gut cast, and select as flies a small grey spider, a teal, and a woodcock. There is a hazel bush in front, with the current running under it; let us try a cast above it, for big fish often lurk there and dart upstream to feed. Now cast gently, and don't work your flies at all, but let them float. That first attempt was a bad one; try a shorter line, and remember that you are not a coach driver. There! That was better; keep back and let your flies drift with the current. You had a rise just now; but you struck too late. I am afraid you won't get one there; come down a little further and try a cast into yonder current on the other side . . . Now you have one; keep up the point of your rod and don't get nervous and lose your head. Work him down to where I am with the net, if you can. Here he is, a small trout over half-a-pound, but in this water the large trout are few and far between, so we must be thankful for small mercies.

In the village of Broughton, Buchan's childhood haunt, you can admire the richly stocked and everchanging garden at Beechgrove. And not far away, apart from the natural riches of the countryside, there are three marvels of horticultural and silvicultural science. The fame surrounding the woods of Dawyck goes back centuries. Here, in 1725, the first larch trees in Scotland were planted, and around that time Dr Pennicuik, in his *Shire of Tweeddale* draws attention to a strange natural phenomenon:

Here, in an old Orchard, did herons in my time build their nests upon some old Pear-trees, whereupon in the harvest time are to be seen much fruit growing, and trouts and eels crawling down the Body of the Trees. These fish the Herons take out of the river of the Tweed to their nests, and as they go in at the mouth, so they are seen to squirt out again at the Draught. And this is the remarkable Riddle they so much talk of, to have Flesh, Fish and Fruit at the same time upon one tree.

The orchard and the heronry no longer exist, but Dawyck arboretum, which passed into the ownership of the Royal Botanic Gardens of Edinburgh a few years ago, boasts what must be one of the most comprehensive collections of specimen trees in Britain. The woodlands throughout the Dawyck estate speak of the inspired care and imagination lavished on them for generations, and the arboretum is the zenith of that inheritance.

At Stobo, too, we can reap the rewards of the planning that was implemented

The exquisite Japanese gardens at Stobo Castle. They are particularly noted for their azaleas.

decades ago when the exotic Japanese Water Gardens were laid out at Stobo Castle. Nowadays, they provide one of the therapeutic pleasures offered to guests there, for this imposing edifice, recently in danger of demolition, became the subject of a remarkably enterprising rescue operation. Its once decayed interiors and rotting fabric were restored to their former glory with the help of the Historic Buildings Council, and a luxurious health and beauty spa was established. I can testify to its excellence: after the gruelling 1983 general election, I spent a few days there, enjoying its recuperative and highly disciplined regime.

The road now joins the main thoroughfare from Glasgow to Peebles, passing the county's only surviving medieval church. Stobo church dates from the middle of the twelfth century and retains a good deal of its original character. To the north lies Lyne Water, with the attractive villages of Romannobridge and West Linton, but my journey takes a right hand turn southwards, to the Royal and Ancient Burgh of Peebles.

THREE

PEEBLES FOR PLEASURE

Neidpath Castle rears up high above the approach road to Peebles, an ancient sentinel guarding the entrance to the town. Below its massive, ten-foot walls, the hillside descends sharply to the Tweed, where the river glides through the graceful arches of a disused nineteenth-century railway bridge.

From Neidpath's courtyard, in 1303, the immortal Scots patriot William Wallace rode out with his ally Sir Simon Fraser, whose family then owned the castle. On that day they shared a famous victory at Roslin Moor over the 'Hammer of the Scots', the English King Edward I; later, Simon Fraser shared his leader's fate at the hands of the vengeful king. Like Wallace, the Peeblesshire resistance leader was hanged, drawn and quartered in London and his remains sent back for exhibition in Scotland as a grisly but ineffective warning to those who would emulate him.

But the castle's own history is remarkably unbloody. Only once was it taken by an opposing army: in 1650 it was surrendered to Cromwell's troops when threatened with bombardment from across the Tweed. But even on this occasion, the greatest outrage committed by the attackers seems to have been the stabling of their horses in the twelfth-century church of St Andrew's nearby, of which only the tower now remains. The castle has stood the ravages of time remarkably well, however, and its grounds have to a large extent recovered from the wanton vandalism of the reprobate fourth Duke of Queensberry, who at the end of the eighteenth century, and as an act of spite against his heir, denuded the castle of its surrounding trees and destroyed its terraces. Among the victims were magnificent beeches and venerable yews. But subsequent generations have made good the folly of 'Old Q', and the sight of Neidpath now on a crisp autumn day would surely gladden the eyes of Wordsworth, whose outrage at the felling of Neidpath's glories evoked the famous lines:

Degenerate Douglas! Oh, the unworthy lord
Whose mean despite of heart could so far please,
And love of havoc (for with such disease
Fame taxes him), that he could send forth word
To level with the dust a noble horde,
A brotherhood of venerable trees.

OPPOSITE *The mighty walls of Neidpath Castle, owned by the Earl of Wemyss and March, have dominated this stretch of the Tweed for seven centuries.*

41

The castle is, of course, celebrated in verse by many local poets, but the piece of its history which captured the imagination of both Walter Scott and Thomas Campbell was the tragic tale of the Douglas daughter who pined and died for love of the young Laird of Tushielaw. I like the succinctness of Cambell's version:

Earl March looked on his dying child,
And, smit with grief to view her –
The youth, he cried, whom I exiled
Shall be restored to woo her.

She's at her window many an hour,
His coming to discover:
And he looked up to Ellen's bower
And she looked on her lover –

Just below Neidpath, this fine viaduct bears testimony to the days when an extensive railway network spanned the area.

The Royal and Ancient Burgh of Peebles. The burghs originated as self-governing bodies of local craftsmen and merchants, granted lands and privileges by charter in the Middle Ages.

But ah! so pale, he knew her not
Though her smile was on him dwelling –
And am I then forgot – forgot?
It broke the heart of Ellen.

In vain he weeps, in vain he sighs,
Her cheek is cold as ashes,
Nor love's own kiss shall wake those eyes
To lift their silken lashes.

I have a particular affection for Neidpath. At the annual Peebles Beltane Festival, an individual who has contributed to the well-being of the burgh is appointed Warden of that historic keep for the coming year. In 1981 that honour was mine.

All the Border burghs have a long, distinguished, and in many cases royal pedigree – Peebles is generally supposed to have been granted its charter by King David I in the twelfth century – and in all of them, the reorganization of

43

local government in the 1970s, breaking as it did the long tradition of the town councils, was bitterly resented. Local pride and patriotism ride high, and this is especially true during the annual Common Ridings and festivals, which encapsulate the characteristics of the respective towns. Peebles' Beltane festival held in June reflects in particular the town's ancient connections with royalty. It was King Robert the Bruce who first granted the town the right to hold a fair, although in all probability the Beltane ceremonies originated in Celtic times. The advent of Christianity changed the nature of the celebrations from heathen worship to sport and pleasure, and by the time James I, Scotland's poet-king, came to know and love Peebles, revellers were flocking to the town from far and wide. James I's poem 'Peebles to the Play' is a classic description of his subjects at their leisure; but one must also wonder whether the King, seeing the young men and women enjoying themselves, did not pass a regretful thought for his own youth, spent in imprisonment in England. The ultimate seal of royal approval came from the sixth James, whose charter proclaiming the Beltane Fair is still read out at the celebrations today. Appropriately, the annual festival, which had lapsed for some years, was reinstated to mark the diamond jubilee celebrations for Queen Victoria.

The two main events of the festival are the Riding of the Marches, the common thread running through all Border festivals (as described in later chapters) and the crowning of the Beltane queen in the presence of her court. The chosen queen is aged about twelve and her court consists of every primary school child in the town. She has white-robed maids of honour, kilted highlandmen, satin-breeched, bewigged courtiers, a miniature naval guard and subjects appropriate to a monarch of such tender years: children from other

All that remains of ancient St Andrews' Church in Peebles is the tower, restored in the nineteenth century by William Chambers.

lands, from history, nursery rhyme and legend, and – from the animal kingdom – six-year-old children in the shape of grey mice. The ceremony is stiff with protocol, from the time the fair is proclaimed at the town cross, through to the colourful procession of children along the High Street to take up their positions on the wide steps of the parish church, the arrival of the queen in a horsedrawn carriage and the reading of the many good wishes from the friends of the Beltane festival overseas. Year after year it follows the pattern laid down by those imaginative Victorians who conceived it to mark their own queen's Jubilee.

For the rest of the year Peebles is a modest, contented town, providing quiet enjoyments. Native Peebleans, known as 'Gutterbluids' as opposed to incoming 'Stooryfits' (Dustyfeet), are not afraid to sing its praises. A nineteenth-century gentleman from Peebles, after a grand tour of Europe, breathed his native air contentedly and uttered the oft-repeated phrase: 'Paris is a' very weel, but gie me Peebles for Pleasure.'

The confident assertion in *Chambers Encyclopedia* that 'the Tweed is the noblest of all Scottish rivers' is also the statement of a Peebles man. William Chambers, born in the town in 1800, endured great poverty when he was young. His motto, 'He who tholes overcomes', was born out of his own experience. 'Thole' is a word for which there is no exact English equivalent: to endure hardship, or discomfort, I suppose, comes near. A kind of Scottish Dick Whittington, Chambers left his native town for Edinburgh at the age of thirteen, where he became apprenticed to a publisher, and later, with his younger brother Robert, he founded the famous Chambers publishing firm. He even became Lord Provost of Edinburgh; but in spite of riches and success he never forgot his early poverty, and under his guidance steps were taken in

A smart line-up at the Peebles sheep-dog trials.

45

Edinburgh to improve some of the more squalid slums. At the end of his illustrious career, he returned to Peebles, and has left as a legacy to the town the handsome set of public rooms, art gallery and library which bear his name, and also his scholarly and definitive *History of Peeblesshire*.

But the placidity of Peebles has not been uninterrupted. In spite of King James VI's granting of the Beltane Fair charter, it was reported during his reign that 'The king has not in all his realm such troublesome subjects as those in Peebles'. And although Lord Cockburn coined the phrase in the eighteenth century, 'As quiet as the grave – or Peebles', the active spirits of the town were to the fore again a hundred years later. The 1884 election, the first fought under universal male suffrage, saw the return of Sir Charles Tennant as the Liberal MP for the area, but not before Peebles was convulsed with such rioting that it was singled out in the *Illustrated London News* for comment on the rowdy behaviour of its citizens.

Sir Graham Montgomery and his two sons were also mobbed and bespattered with dirt, but although stones were freely thrown about, no serious injuries to persons were recorded ... In the evening, the election of Mr Tennant was celebrated with much rejoicing. There was a torchlight procession, and effigies of some individuals were burnt.

There is a long tradition of radical politics in this part of the Borders. Sir Charles Tennant, MP at the end of the last century, was also Asquith's father-in-law, and his great house and estate at the Glen, near Peebles, was a regular meeting place for members of the Liberal Cabinets during summer recesses.

A later MP for the old constituency of Selkirkshire and Peeblesshire was Sir Donald Maclean, who retained his seat in the Liberal debacle after the First World War. Since Asquith himself had been defeated, Sir Donald stepped into the breach and became leader of the parliamentary party, a post he held with great distinction and which he gracefully relinquished on Asquith's return to the Commons. Canvassing for election in the early 1960s, I called on many houses in Peebles where I was regaled with memories of Sir Donald – and also of his son of the same name who defected to Russia with Guy Burgess. And in one Peeblesshire village a nonogenarian greeted me with the words, 'I'm very pleased to meet you, young man – the last Member of Parliament I shook hands with was Mr Gladstone'!

If Neidpath Castle, symbolizing the distant past, guards one end of Peebles, a testament to the town's recent evolution stands at the other in the majestic shape of the Hydro Hotel. While Peebles abounds now in good hotels, three are of particular interest: the Hydro, reminiscent of Victorian health-seekers, which nowadays flourishes as a small conference centre; the Tontine Hotel in the High Street, whose origins are enshrined in its name (founded as a group venture, it was destined to become the property of the longest survivor); and the Cross Keys Inn in the Northgate, the original of the Cleikum Inn of Sir Walter Scott's novel *St Ronan's Well*.

46

An interlocking pattern of fields around Ladyuard Hill, near Peebles.

LEFT *The view to Ladyuard Hill, near Beggerpath Bridge.*

47

FOUR

LEITHEN WATER TO GALA WATER

One of the delights of travelling around the Borders is that there are frequently several alternative routes between two set points, offering different but equally charming perspectives. Thus, from Peebles to Innerleithen you can take the main road which runs along the left bank of the Tweed, with plenty of stopping places for anglers and others, and presenting the opportunity to enjoy one of the graded walks in Glentress Forest. Or there is the back road on the Tweed's right bank, past the water gardens and wildfowlery of Kailzie, the forest of Cardrona, and the possibility of a detour to the ancient and picturesque Traquair Kirk. It is this road that leads directly to the oldest inhabited house in Scotland.

The original main gates of Traquair House, flanked by stone bears from the family's coat of arms, stand shut, as they have done for over two centuries. This is no act of unfriendliness, nor an indication of decay, for Traquair must be one of the most vibrant and welcoming of Scotland's historic houses. The closed gates are a reminder of that romantic loser, Bonnie Prince Charlie, and the support given to his cause by the fifth Earl of Traquair. Charles Edward Stuart, like so many of his royal forebears, received hospitality here, and as he left on his unsuccessful quest for power, the gates were shut behind him with the Earl's vow that they would not be reopened till the Stuarts were restored to the throne. So the visitor must bypass the Bear Gates, with their avenue of mighty trees stretching towards the house, and enter Traquair by a side gate.

Fifteen generations of the Stuarts of Traquair have stamped their personality on the house; they have played in important part in public life, and they have acted as host to no fewer than twenty-seven kings and queens. The house itself traces that tripartite story of domestic continuity, public duty and royal association. On display are family letters, diaries and housekeeping accounts – and the rosary and crucifix of Mary Queen of Scots, whose escape from Holyrood after the murder of Rizzio was aided by the faithful Laird of Traquair. There is the bed she slept in, covered with her own needlework, and the cradle of the infant King James VI. And the central and romantic part played by the Earls of Traquair during the Jacobite Risings of 1715 and 1745 is commemorated not just in the sad optimism of those closed gates but in the collection of glass engraved with Jacobite verses and symbols in which secret and solemn toasts were drunk.

OPPOSITE *Magnificent beech woods near the village of Stow.*

49

The family's adherence to Roman Catholicism had cost it dear in the previous century, when in 1688 a mob from Peebles ransacked the house and stripped it of all Popish articles, which they then burned publicly. The room in which Mass was celebrated not only provided the best lookout point; it also adjoins a secret staircase. The chapel attached to the house dates only from the coming of Catholic emancipation in the mid-nineteenth century.

Traquair today, under the inspired guidance of the twentieth laird, Peter Maxwell-Stuart, and his wife Flora, has enthusiastically come to terms with present-day demands. The old brewery might have remained merely an interesting museum piece, but instead it is a working brewery which produced real ale in limited quantities even in the 1960s, before real ale had really been thought of, let alone become a campaigning point. The buildings clustering near the house, once part of the complicated and extensive substructure required to keep such a place going, could have been allowed to fall into ruins; instead they house a lively community of artists and craftsmen who produce high quality goods for sale at Traquair and elsewhere. Throughout the summer there is a succession of craft fairs, antique fairs and plant fairs, but the main fiesta, held on the first weekend of August, is without parallel in the region and probably in the country. Not only do craftworkers gather to sell their wares, and the occasional pressure group to push its pamphlets, but fringe theatre groups on their way to the Edinburgh Festival congregate in every corner of the grounds: buskers, musicians, puppeteers, mime artists and performers of all kinds provide a glorious informal demonstration of their own particular talents.

The Stuarts of Traquair were important political figures in the seventeenth

At Kailzie, on the road from Peebles to Traquair, extensive gardens and a wildfowlery have been developed, along with other attractions with the tourist in mind.

and eighteenth centuries, and the house was then a nerve-centre of activity and influence. But they backed the wrong horse in the politico-religious divides, and not only did their power diminish but so did their lands and wealth. The result is that the house, substantially unchanged since then, gives us a much clearer idea of life two or three hundred years ago than houses where Georgian, Victorian or Edwardian prosperity has obliterated the evidence of the relatively simple and more indigenous architectural styles of earlier times.

From the nearby town of Innerleithen – smallest of all the Border burghs before their abolition – and from the neighbouring village of Walkerburn, high quality knitwear is sent all over the world, supplying the luxury markets of Europe, America, Japan, Hong Kong, Africa and the Middle East. Of all towns in Britain, Innerleithen boasts the highest export earnings figure per head of population. While it is true that the woollen industry in the Borders – which I will examine in greater detail in later chapters – has declined since the days when it was universally pre-eminent, at the top end of the market its hold is as firm as ever. While other countries compete now with cheaper fabrics and lower rates, the fine craftsmanship of the Border millworkers, the enterprising fashion designers and energetic sales forces ensure that for quality wear, the firms that have their base in Innerleithen, Hawick and the other mill towns, are still unequalled.

In the Clan Royal mill shop in Walkerburn is a small museum which traces the progress of wool through its various stages of production, and examines the development of the industry from its origins in the cottage weaving business to its present industrialization. The museum commemorates, too, the great

The oldest inhabited house in Scotland, Traquair has been home to twenty generations of the same family, and has welcomed twenty-seven kings and queens to its doors.

record-breaking effort in 1976 when the whole process – clipping, washing, dying, spinning, knitting, stitching and making up – was reduced to the remarkable time of four hours forty minutes, from sheep's back to man's back.

I have already mentioned Scott's novel *St Ronan's Well*, and the 'Well' of the title is to be found at Innerleithen. (St Ronan was a saint of the Celtic Church, and his connection with the town owed everything to Scott's imagination.) The waters were claimed to be particularly effective for eye and skin disorders in the second half of the eighteenth century, and their flavour of brimstone was accounted for by the fact that the Devil had bathed in the spring! In fact its main components are salt and lime chloride.

Both Walkerburn and Innerleithen are very much small industrial towns. Walkerburn, though, has one surprising listed building – a cast-iron pissoir in the main street.

Leaving these communities behind, we return to Ettrick and Lauderdale, to the solitude of the Tweed valley and the wooded hills that border it. On the south bank of the river are small mansions typical of Peeblesshire – the late Georgian house of Holylee is a particularly attractive example – and on the north bank is the old tower of Elibank and the more recent house of that name. It has now passed out of the hands of its hereditary owners. A Murray of Elibank was in Asquith's Cabinet, and another stood with Wolfe on the heights of Quebec, and afterwards became the first Governor-General of Canada.

But if these scions of that ancient family found fame and prestige in the wider world, in the Borders it is their ancestor, Sir Gideon Murray, who made the family name great. He it was who built the old tower in the sixteenth century, and who became the father-in-law of Will Scott of Harden. Will, a high spirited young man who had inherited his father Wat's reiving instincts, embarked on a raid of Elibank's cattle. Sir Gideon apprehended him, and, having no love for the Scotts, prepared to hang him summarily. Lady Murray intervened. It would, she pointed out, be a dreadful waste of an upstanding young laird when there were three ill-favoured and unmarried Murray daughters for whom husbands must be found. Will Scott was given the choice of 'the wife or the wuddy' – marriage with the youngest and plainest Murray daughter, 'muckle-mouthed Meg', or the gallows. He rejected Meg without so much as setting eyes on her, and prepared for his fate. At the last minute, however, discretion overcame valour, and he accepted the offer of Meg's hand. Whatever her physical shortcomings, she more than made up for them with other qualities and the marriage was a highly successful one. From this union, in another few generations, sprang Sir Walter Scott.

Their famous descendant spent seven happy years at Ashiestiel, the house next to Elibank, when he was first appointed Sheriff of Selkirk. From here he would ride out in search of the disappearing Border ballads and folklore, and here he composed his great poetic works, 'The Lay of the Last Minstrel', 'Marmion', and 'The Lady of the Lake'.

A rather bad statue of Scott stands outside the inn at Clovenfords. (Surely

One of the stone bears at the entrance gates to Traquair.

no-one in the whole history of Scotland has been so often portrayed in stone, in marble, in oils and in pencil!) Before he moved to Ashiestiel, Scott often stayed at Clovenfords and it was here too that the Wordsworths came, when Dorothy begged her brother to 'turn aside and view the braes of Yarrow'. That he did not do so then continued to haunt him on his later visits, for his sister had died in the meantime and so was never to see the valley that inspired her imagination.

Like so many other villages in the Borders, Clovenfords stands a little way away from the parish church and school. They bear the name of Caddonfoot for it is the Caddon Water that meanders gently through the village on its way to the Tweed. Of all villages in the Borders, it has seen the greatest physical change since I have known it. Well situated both for those who work in Galashiels and for the employees of the nearby Peel Hospital, it has a substantial council housing development and a large number of new private houses too. But the vineries, for which it was once famous, are no more, victims of the soaring fuel costs of recent years.

53

Clovenfords Inn was an old staging post, and it is the old stagecoach road which takes us across the hills to the village of Stow. The road continues up the Gala Water, another tributary of the Tweed, via Fountainhall and Heriot: the main A7 that is now the trunk route on the other bank dates only from the beginning of the nineteenth century. This stretch of the road, and other major works in the Borders such as the 'Duke's Dyke' which surrounds Floors Castle at Kelso, were built by French prisoners during the Napoleonic Wars. The presence of these men in the Border towns from about 1811 to 1814 requires an explanation.

In most of the towns where they were billeted, a parole system operated. They stayed in local lodgings, and initially there was a feeling of hostility to the involuntary guests (the self-styled 'gentry' of Selkirk held a meeting before their arrival at which it was decided to ostracize the French). In time, though, opinion must have mellowed – certainly among the womenfolk of the towns. There are records in both Peebles and Selkirk of illegitimate children born to French officers. It is not difficult to imagine what a stir these men would have caused – they seem to have been a high-spirited group who were not afraid to find their own amusements. In Selkirk they established a café and a theatre, and, according to the testimony of one of their number who later recorded his reminiscences, parted on good terms with their hosts. The people of Selkirk appear to have treated them kindly, and although there were frequent breaches of the one-mile curfew limit, no prisoner was ever reported on. In Jedburgh, their experience was much less happy: I would hazard a guess that this was due to the

PREVIOUS PAGES *The sun sets over Stantling Craig reservoir, in the hills between Clovenfords and Stow.*

The ivy-covered ruins of the ancient church of St Mary of Wedale at Stow.

56

fact that they were lodged not with the townspeople in private accommodation but in the prison.

The old road runs parallel to the now overgrown track of that other tribute to nineteenth-century engineering, the Waverley railway line which ran from Edinburgh to Carlisle – one of the most scenic routes in the entire UK rail network. In 1969 the railway closed, a victim of Lord Beeching's plan, and now the roads provide the only thoroughfares through the Borders.

Stow was not just a stop on the main line. In the heyday of the railways a branch line ran from it to Lauder. A well-to-do but servantless lady of Edwardian days alighted from the train at Stow and approached the station-master. 'Can you assist me to the Lauder train, my man?' 'It's ower the brig to Lauder', came the reply. 'But I need assistance. I have a tin chest,' she appealed to him. 'I dinna care whether you've a tin chest or a brass arse – it's ower the brig to Lauder.'

Alas! the grass grows over the railway now, and no sign remains of the footbridge, but there is an attractive ruined bridge in Stow known as the packhorse bridge. Although it is sometimes reputed to date back to Roman times, it was in fact built in the seventeenth century, some time after 1632. In that year a meeting of heritors (property owners) was called in Stow. It was decided to build a bridge in order to encourage church attendance and give backsliders no excuse, for when the Gala rose the people on the far side of the stream had claimed that they were unable, because of floods, to attend the services.

Stow has a particularly fine parish church, and a strong tradition associated with it. St Mary's of Wedale was one of the churches granted a right of sanctuary by Malcolm VI, and was reputed to have been founded after King Arthur had brought a piece of the true cross to Wedale – the old name for Gala Water. 'Wedale' is reputed to derive from 'Vale of Woe' and Stow to be the site of a great Arthurian battle. For the Arthurian legend is strong in the Borders, with the Eildon Hills claimed as the sleeping place of the legendary king and his knights, and Drumelzier in Peeblesshire as the site of Merlin's grave.

The smaller of the two ruins near Stow church is known as the Bishop's Palace, where the Bishop of St Andrews stayed on his visits to this, the remotest point of his diocese. Although I refer to Stow as a village, it was in fact raised to the status of a burgh in 1669, and claims a town hall rather than a village hall. The ceremony of becoming a burgess often had strange traditions associated with it in the past, and in Stow a new burgessman was required at one time to wear the 'Stow Hat', an enormous cocked hat with a foot-wide brim.

The Stow fair provided a meeting place between Edinburgh and the Borders in the late eighteenth and early nineteenth centuries, and nowadays Stow is within commuting distance of Edinburgh, as are the villages further north on the Gala Water. But we strike eastward now, across the common lands once bitterly disputed by the people of Wedale and the monks of Melrose, towards the Royal and Ancient Burgh of Lauder.

FIVE

LAUDERDALE

An unsuspecting traveller on the A68, planning to make his way through Lauder on the first Saturday of August, will find his passage impeded in a way he may well find bewildering. Hundreds of horsemen, whose leader bears a large banner in his hand, head a procession through streets lined with onlookers. Bands follow the riders, and behind them are troops of townspeople, singing and dancing along the broad High Street. This is Lauder Common Riding in full swing. Although, before I came here, I was aware of the existence and the general pattern of the Border Common Ridings, I was not prepared for their emotional impact. The Lauder version does not have the unbroken tradition of Selkirk, Hawick or Langholm, but it is the first that we come to on this route so I will give a brief description of Common Ridings here and return to them in more detail in later chapters. Although Peebles has its Riding of the Marches as part of the Beltane festival, the focus of attention then is directed towards the crowning of the Beltane queen, while at Innerleithen the St Ronan's Games, initiated by Scott and Hogg, have no equestrian element.

During the 1930s and 1940s those Border towns which did not have Common Ridings introduced festivals, so that now each town has its own. Galashiels has its Braw Lads' Gathering, Kelso its Civic Week, Melrose and Jedburgh their festivals. But the Common Ridings proper stretch back centuries. In times past, the towns were granted charters to hold annual fairs, and at one of these the burgesses (those who held property in the towns) made an inspection of the boundaries of the common lands surrounding and held by the town as part of their charter. An unchecked encroachment by a land-hungry neighbour might become a permanent nuisance.

Eventually the fairs diminished in importance. After the Reformation the sort of display of public enjoyment they would have occasioned was discouraged, though to link some sort of festivity to a necessary procedure was acceptable. The Riding of the Marches survived in certain towns, and in time the mounted procession came to be led not by the provost of the burgh but by a young man known as the Cornet. Into his care the burgh flag is entrusted by the provost, who adjures him to carry it round the marches and return it 'unsullied and untarnished'.

This is the core of the ritual, which all Common Ridings share. Around it

OPPOSITE *The imperious eagle at the entrance to Thirlestane Castle symbolizes the power wielded by the mighty Duke of Lauderdale in the seventeenth century.*

59

each town has woven its own traditional variations, and from early June until mid-August there is always one town in the Borders celebrating in its own style, with ceremonials, dinners, sporting events, concerts, dances and, of course, the 'ride-outs'.

I know of nowhere where riding is so universal as in the Borders. Here it is not the esoteric sport of horse-mad little girls, and though there is much good hunting, racing and eventing, the enthusiastic and basic skills you see at the Common Ridings are of a different genre. Men, women, and children from all walks of life take part, and as you see the company of over four hundred following the Lauder Cornet, Bishop Ross's comment on their forebears echoes down through four centuries: 'A very poor man they deem it to be without a horse.'

Lauder, like Peebles, Jedburgh and Selkirk is a Royal and Ancient Burgh. (Or should one say 'was' in these days of newly designated districts and regions?) The Common Riding, at any rate, brings it to life as such again. But Lauder's associations with royalty have not always been happy, as its part in the history of that unsuitable king, James III, testifies. Of an artistic and peace-loving temperament, he made the mistake of surrounding himself not with ambitious and uncouth nobles, but with lowly-born architects, musicians and artists, a clique with whom he felt at ease and with whom he was – tragically – able to forget about the responsibilities of government.

The resentment of his nobles at their king's preoccupation with his favourites had reached a peak by the time the court encamped at Lauder in 1482. They met in Lauder Kirk to plan the destruction of the men they saw as rivals. But who would take the initiative? One of the nobles likened the meeting to a group of mice deciding which of their number would place a bell round the neck of a marauding cat: 'Which of us will bell the cat?' The Earl of Angus promptly volunteered, earning himself the sobriquet of Archibald Bell-the-Cat till the

A proud day for the Lauder Cornet, as he carries the burgh flag at the head of his followers.

ABOVE *A mounted supporter of the Lauder cornet.*

end of his days. The cats were indeed belled. They were hanged over Lauder Brig, in full view of their distressed sovereign.

The pink-washed church which stands in Lauder today is a later building, dating from 1673. It is a unique design by the great architect Sir William Bruce. It takes the form of a Greek cross with a small central tower, and I am not surprised that it is the only example of its kind: its architectural interest is well redressed by its acoustic difficulties. Lauder Kirk's later renovations have carefully followed the original style, and it retains its box pews. The old Tolbooth, which stands across the road from the church, dates back to the fourteenth century, though this is not the original structure. It has been rebuilt several times, but always in the same style, and the building which now straddles the unspoilt High Street of Lauder is very similar to the one at which rents were paid by local traders, tolls collected from passing travellers, and ne'er-do-wells incarcerated over the centuries. Now the cells are used as a language school, and the hall was used for meetings of Lauder Town Council until the Council was abolished in the reorganization of local government.

Lauder, which is reputed to have the most unspoilt pre-Victorian high street in Scotland, never achieved the status of a manufacturing town during the Industrial Revolution, as some of its neighbours did. It was never, therefore, in the hands of philanthropic Victorian mill-owners who so well-meaningly but often so ill-advisedly replaced old buildings with monuments to their riches. The streets and back lanes of Lauder today conform very closely with the pattern laid out in medieval times.

But if the town has changed little, Thirlestane Castle (originally know as Lauder Castle) just outside the town has been drastically altered over the centuries. It is the seat of the Maitland family, the Earls of Lauderdale, whose prominence in Scottish politics was at its peak in the sixteenth and seventeenth centuries. From this family came Queen Mary's Secretary of State, Maitland of

Lauder High Street lined with spectators as the last of the riders at the burgh's Common Riding return to town.

ABOVE *The well-earned break for horses and riders at the 'Watering Stane'.*

Lethington, a skilled and devious politician, known popularly as 'Michael Wily' – a corruption of Machiavelli. His brother, Chancellor to James VI, settled the family at Thirlestane. He it was who transformed the basic fort which already existed into a solid and comfortable square mansion with turrets at each corner. This is the core of the modern, much enlarged T-shaped house which we see today. The major alterations were carried out under the castle's best known occupant, the only Duke of Lauderdale. The Duke, or second Earl in his early days, was a supporter of the Solemn League and Covenant against King Charles I; but later his Royalist sympathies got the better of his Presbyterian ones, and he changed sides. He followed Charles II into exile in Holland, returned with him and was captured at the Battle of Worcester, and spent some time under sentence of death in the Tower of London. However, he was saved by the Restoration. Thereafter, Lauderdale became one of Charles's closest confidants, and the absolute ruler on his behalf in Scotland. He was a man utterly corrupted by power: from being a principled advocate of the freedom of worship of the Scottish people and an upholder of the royal cause in troubled times, he descended, when given authority, to a course of unscrupulous self-preservation and repression which eventually lost him the support of Parliament, the Privy Council, and ultimately the King.

But there is one episode in the life of the notorious Duke which redeems him a little. One of his tenants, Thomas Hardie of Midside of Tollishill, had experienced a particularly hard winter. He had no money when the term-day – the date on which rents were due – drew close, and feared eviction and destitution for himself and his young wife, Maggie. But that resourceful young woman went to plead their cause before Lauderdale himself. Impressed by her beauty and courage, he did not reject her plea out of hand. He asked instead for the seemingly impossible: as a token of the frosts and snows she blamed for her husband's plight, she was to bring, in lieu of rent, a snowball in June. Maggie used her ingenuity, and in a sheltered burnside hollow, she packed a crevice tight with snow, and covered the entrance against the light of day. In June, her improvized deep-freeze yielded up its contents. The Earl (his dukedom came later) kept his word on delivery of the snowball, and absolved Maggie and her husband of their arrears of rent.

Thereafter the Hardies prospered, and the Earl's fortunes declined. But although he had many enemies he had, in the Hardies, two devoted admirers. During his period of exile and imprisonment they put aside the rent due to him, and eventually Maggie determined to take it to the captive and destitute Lauderdale. She baked the gold sovereigns in a cake and, disguised as a boy, set off for London with Thomas. At the Tower she presented the cake to the astonished Lauderdale, who made use of the coins on his escape to Holland. When, on Charles's restoration, the Duke of Lauderdale returned to his own home, he did not forget Maggie. She and her children received free rent of Tollishill for life, and the silver girdle with which he presented her may still be seen in the National Museum of Antiquities in Edinburgh.

OPPOSITE *This view of Thirlestane Castle shows the different stages of its development: the original house of Chancellor Maitland, the Restoration extensions of the Duke of Lauderdale, and the more recent wings, giving the building its 'T' formation.*

But this episode apart, self-interest was his ruling passion. So ambitious a man was bound to find himself dissatisfied with the relative modesty of Chancellor Maitland's castle at Thirlestane, but fortunately his architectural tastes were more reliable than his political instincts. He commissioned Sir William Bruce – responsible for the extensions to Holyrood Palace as well as Lauder Kirk (was the latter a by-product of his employment at the castle?) – to draw up plans. He employed only the best craftsmen, servants of the King and specialists from Europe, and the result is an interior of amazing baroque splendour.

The final alterations were made in the nineteenth century, but the last decade has played a no less distinguished role in the appearance of the castle. In 1972, when the present owner, the Hon. Gerald Maitland-Carew inherited Thirlestane, the fabric of the building had deteriorated to an appalling extent. There were forty separate outbreaks of dry rot, the foundations were crumbling, and the ornate plaster ceilings were badly damaged. That the building, in the four-year period from 1978 to 1982, was fully restored to its seventeenth-century splendour, is the result of teamwork between skilled architects and craftsmen, dedicated owners, and supportive government departments. As part of Thirlestane's regeneration, one wing now houses the Border Country Life Museum. Here there are not only displays devoted to life in the region in times past, but source material for local historians, and exhibition space for artists and craftsmen.

Earlston village, a few miles from Lauder, is famous as the birthplace of the legendary Thomas the Rhymer. True Thomas, or Thomas of Ercildoune (Earlston) as he was otherwise known, was no ordinary poet. Born in the early thirteenth century, legend tells us that he was seduced by the Queen of Elfland, who lured him away to her own regions for seven years, during which he was to remain silent on pain of never returning to the land of mortal men. Here, in the ballad collected and added to by Scott, she points out to him three roads:

> Oh see ye not yon narrow road
>   So thick beset with thorns and briers?
> That is the path of righteousness,
>   Though after it but few enquires.
>
> And see ye not yon braid braid road
>   That lies across yon lily leven
> That is the path of wickedness
>   Though some call it the road to heaven.
>
> And see ye not that bonny road
>   That winds about the fernie brae?
> That is the road to fair Elfland
>   Where you and I this night maun gae.

Thomas returned from Elfland with the gift of prophecy, and allegedly foretold much of Scotland's history. Although the glen from which he was

Classical Georgian architecture at its most perfect : Mellerstain House, from its elegant gardens.

spirited away by the Elfin queen lies near Melrose, it is Earlston with which he is more intimately associated. An ancient crumbling tower – the Rhymers Tower – stands close to the main road, and at the church at Earlston is an inscribed tablet which is popularly known as the Rhymer's Stone. Thomas the Rhymer was a real-life character, but a rational explanation of the legends surrounding him and his prophecies has never been attempted so far as I am aware. (The Rhymer's family name was Learmonth, and the nineteenth-century Russian poet Lermontov claimed descent from him.)

Lauder and Earlston, together with the villages of Oxton to the north, and smaller settlements such as Dryburgh, Mertoun and Redpath, were all part of Berwickshire until the district boundaries were redrawn. At the last election they fell for the first time within my constituency, while on the uttermost boundary, six miles beyond Earlston, the fine Georgian house of Mellerstain also moved, figuratively speaking, from Berwickshire to Ettrick and Lauderdale. If Thirlestane is the supreme example of grand domestic Restoration architecture, Mellerstain is Georgian building at its most perfect. Designed by the great Adams, father and son, it must rank as one of their finest creations. It was built in two stages: strangely enough the wings, designed by William Adam, came first in 1725, and the bold central block was the later creation of his son. The interior is almost entirely the work of Robert Adam, and in Mellerstain's exquisite library Adam ceilings reach their zenith.

Complementing the classical simplicity of the mansion itself are the gardens, which date from the beginning of this century. They fall in a series of terraces to a loch at the foot of the slope in front of the house, leading the eye to the natural beauty of the Cheviot Hills on the horizon.

The story of the Baillies of Mellerstain and the Earls of Haddington, whose property Mellerstain has been for most of its history, can be traced through family portraits by the finest painters of the time. An original copy of the National Covenant of 1638 testifies to the Baillies' support for the bond formed by Scottish Presbyterians to defend their religion.

In her teens, Lady Grisell Baillie, whose husband George commissioned the first stage of the building of the house, became one of the great heroines of her day. A daughter of the Humes of Marchmont, she managed to keep her father concealed in the crypt of Polwarth church for several days, smuggling food to him without the knowledge of the other members of the family. His pursuers were in full cry, and discovery would have meant death; but the eighteen-year-old girl kept her head and saved her father's. It was while sharing his exile in Holland that she met George Baillie, and returned as his wife to Mellerstain on the restoration of the Hume and Baillie estates. Now, after nearly three centuries, she smiles at us from her portrait, strong, serene and unmarked by the eventful sixty years of her life that had passed when the painting was made.

Of all the mementoes of past generations, the one which takes my fancy most is a tapestry on a wall of the green bedroom. Worked by Elizabeth Baillie in 1771, it bears this sentiment:

> Is there an evil worse than fear itself
> And what avails it that indulgent heaven
> From mortal eyes has wrapt the woes to come
> If we, ingenious to torment ourselves
> Grow pale at hideous fictions of our own?
>
> Enjoy the present, nor with needless care
> Of what may spring from blind misfortune's womb
> Appall the surest hour that life bestows.
> Serene and master of yourself prepare
> For what may come, and leave the rest to heaven.

Mellerstain continues to reflect the interests of its owners. Lord Binning, heir to the Earl of Haddington, who lives here now, is a vintage car enthusiast, and the rally which is held here at the beginning of June attracts vehicles and their owners, myself included, from all over the country.

SIX

SIR WALTER SCOTT

From Mellerstain, Kelso is only a short distance away, but I propose that we make our way there by a circuitous route, taking in the haunts of the Borders' favourite son along the way. It must already be obvious that the influence of Sir Walter Scott permeates almost every town and every byway of the region. Our paths will cross his again, particularly at his home in Abbotsford, and on the bench in Selkirk; but this detour takes us both to his childhood haunts at Smailholm and to his resting place at Dryburgh Abbey.

Walter Scott was born in 1771, not in the Borders but in Edinburgh. As we have already seen, he was the descendant on his father's side of the famous reiver Wat o' Harden and the Flower of Yarrow, and of their son Will Scott who married muckle-mouthed Meg of Elibank. His mother, a Rutherford, had in her veins the blood of two old Border families, the Haliburtons and the Swintons. Walter Scott's father was an Edinburgh solicitor, and his mother the daughter of an Edinburgh professor. At the time of Walter Scott's birth, the capital was beginning to bubble with the fermentation that gave Scotland a golden age of learning. Had he been a robust child, he would no doubt have spent his formative years there, and his life might then have unfolded differently. But he was a weak child of a large family, several of whom had died in infancy. At eighteen months it seems that he contracted polio, which left him with a permanent limp. It was small wonder, then, that his mother felt that the boy's best interests would be served by sending him to the fresh air of his grandfather's farm at Sandyknowe, where he would have the undivided attention of his aunt Janet. So here at Sandyknowe, in the shadow of Smailholm Tower, the child's future was shaped. His love of the Borders, of the countryside and its antiquated but solid peasant structure, was part of that vision which a happy childhood leaves in the imagination.

In adolescence, a short spell at the grammar school in Kelso sculpted two more monuments in his destiny: he discovered, and read avidly, Bishop Percy's fragmentary collection of Border ballads; and he made friends with James Ballantyne, whose life was to be so inextricably linked with his own.

Young Walter Scott returned to Edinburgh, to follow half-heartedly in his father's footsteps in the law, although as an advocate rather than as a solicitor. 'My profession and I', he wrote in later years, 'came to stand nearly on the same footing which honest Slender consoled himself with having established with

OPPOSITE *Smailholm Tower, whose strategic position commanded three entrances to Scotland. In its shadow, the young Scott's poetic imagination was first stirred.*

69

Mistress Anne Page: "There was no great love between us at the beginning, and it pleased heaven to decrease it on further acquaintance."'

The Scottish bar glittered at that time with brilliant young men, whose talents frequently spilled over into the literary world. Scott was of that circle, yet slightly apart from it, for one major reason. The coterie of clever young advocates was mainly Whig, in tune with the radical and reformist elements active across the political spectrum. Champions of the Rights of Man, they echoed Wordsworth's view of the French Revolution: 'Bliss was it in that dawn to be alive, But to be young was very heaven.' But Scott had already become imbued with romanticism: he wanted to go back rather than forward; he equated reform with revolution. Abstract concepts of equality or justice did not appeal to him: feudalism was his ideal. So it was that he fell out of sympathy not just with his colleagues but also with the radical *Edinburgh Review*, which had published some of his earlier writings.

Already the spell which the Borders had woven around him in childhood was proving irresistible. He spent his spare time travelling the highways and byways of the countryside, learning about its life, picking up folklore and legends, tracking down fragments of the disappearing Border ballads, and amending them as he saw fit with his own verse. In the last year of the century two significant events occurred. He renewed his aquaintance with James Ballantyne, now publisher of the *Kelso Mail*, and together they agreed to produce a small volume of the old ballads – *The Minstrelsy of the Scottish Border*, that wonderful collection which, despite Margaret Laidlaw's doubts, captured for us a heritage which might otherwise have been lost. And in the same year he was appointed Sheriff of Selkirk. These two steps bound his future forever closer to

The Queen of Elfland rides to entrap True Thomas: one of Ann Carrick's intricate miniature figures at Smailhom Tower.

the Borders than to Edinburgh. The ballads were to him not just the purest and most dramatic form of folk literature; they represented a way of life which had touched his spirit. They were his political and personal credo, upholding above all the virtures of honour, loyalty and duty to the clan.

In 1804 came Scott's move to Ashiestiel, and the next year saw the publication of his first great creative work 'The Lay of the Last Minstrel'. It was, he wrote to Wordsworth, 'Written with heart and goodwill, and for no other reason than to discharge my mind of the ideas which from infancy have rushed upon it.' It guaranteed him fame outside the talented Edinburgh meritocracy: he became a popular poet overnight.

John Buchan, in his excellent and percipient biography, sums up Scott's attitude at the time thus: 'He had no desire for literary fame … a Border laird was his ideal rather than a distinguished man of letters, but a Border laird must have an agreeable hobby to fill his time and money to support his dignity.' Before ten years had passed, three things had changed inexorably the course of Scott's destiny. He had turned from writing poetry to writing novels. The immediate success of the anonymous *Waverley* and its successors, which was enhanced by the mystery surrounding their authorship (initiated originally because Scott felt that novel-writing conflicted with the dignity of his position as a Clerk at the Court of Session), brought him an unlooked-for source of income. He had given up the lease of Ashiestiel and achieved his ambition of becoming a Border laird by beginning the building of Abbotsford at the spot, between Galashiels and Melrose, known as Clarty Hole. This scheme was originally modest in conception, but a desire for more grandeur, and a land-hunger, got the better of him over the years. And, through the best of motives – a desire to help James Ballantyne – he became fatally embroiled in unwise commercial dealing.

The picture we have of him at the inception of Abbotsford shows him as a completely happy man. He was high in the esteem of his fellow men – 'the world's darling' – and the world beat a track to his door and filled his postbag with correspondence. He had acquired the friendship of his clan chief, the Duke of Buccleuch, and he was given a baronetcy by George IV. He created at Abbotsford his own bastion against the changes in society which were fermenting around him and which he so hated so much. He administered justice at Selkirk Sheriff Court with fairness, commonsense, and a complete under-standing of the human values and frailties of those who appeared before the bench.

But at the end of 1825 disaster struck. The Ballantyne firm, for which Scott was now solely responsible, crashed with debts totalling £130,000. The story of how this came to be is a complicated one; it is the consequence of it that is relevant here. Scott determined not to take the course of bankruptcy, but through his writing to pay his creditors in full: 'My right hand shall pay my debt.' That he did so, and was able to write under such circumstances, 'spinning gold from his entrails', as one contemporary put it, raises him to the rank of hero. He was never free from debt till the end of his life, but his debts were paid.

He died at Abbotsford in 1832, broken in health by worry and by his Herculean efforts, bereaved by the death of his wife and his beloved grandson, and distressed by the inevitability of parliamentary reform ('I really do believe it was reform that killed him', said James Hogg). But he died true to his own code of values, leaving the Borders as influenced by him as he had been by Smailholm Tower in his happy childhood days.

> We have carved him statues in street and square,
> We have carved him a temple rich and rare,
> But the grandest stone to his memory still
> Is a grey-walled tower on the windy hill.

Smailholm Tower today is probably the best preserved and least spoiled of all the peel towers. It lies on the rocky outcrop of Lady Hill on Sandyknowe Farm, over six hundred feet above sea level. What a wonderful situation for carrying the message of the blazing beacons across the countryside in time of trouble! It dates from the sixteenth century, and boasts not only walls five feet thick but the unusual feature of a barrel-vaulted roof, as well as a vaulted room on the ground floor which was typical of the peel towers.

Until recently the interior of Smailholm was a gaping void between the first floor and the vaulted roof. But skilful restoration by the Department of Ancient Monuments has replaced the flooring and renovated the stairs, and the tower now provides a permanent home for a unique and appropriate collection. Ann Carrick and Donald Scott are a husband and wife team of artists who have lived and worked in the Borders for many years. As well as being painters, they have each developed a particular medium of their own: Donald Scott is one of the country's foremost weavers of tapestries; Ann Carrick specializes in costume figures. To call them dolls is to understate them. In 1982 they mounted a joint exhibition of their work inspired by the *Minstrelsy*, and this exhibition was incorporated, in its entirety, into the newly re-opened Smailholm Tower the following year. The figures are exquisitely costumed miniatures of characters from those ballads which Scott so painstakingly preserved, and the tapestries complement the moods of the ballads in abstract designs.

From Smailholm the road winds back towards Dryburgh Abbey. This is Scott's resting place, by virtue not of his worldly achievements, but of his descent from his Haliburton ancestors. There too lies another great Borderer, Earl Haig, whose family seat, Bemersyde, adjoins the grounds of the ruined abbey.

There were four great Border abbeys in medieval times, all of them founded by King David I in the twelfth century, at Dryburgh, Jedburgh, Kelso and Melrose. They were lavishly endowed: one of King David's descendants ruefully referred to him as 'ane sair sanct for the croun', in that he had parted with so much land and property to benefit the Church that the monarchy was thereby impoverished. The abbeys all suffered from the ravages of war and the

Dryburgh Abbey: the tomb of Sir Walter Scott is in the side chapel in the background.

LEFT *The massive statue of Sir William Wallace, near Dryburgh, commissioned in 1814 by the eleventh Earl of Buchan, was the first monument erected in Scotland to her greatest patriot.*

neglect of post-Reformation times, and now stand in varying degrees of ruination. But they still convey some impression of their former glory nonetheless.

The other abbeys stand in towns, part of their history and their sufferings. Dryburgh alone lies in secluded tranquillity among mature cedars, beeches and yews, in a little horseshoe bend of the Tweed. It was founded by the Premonstratensians, or White Canons, and seems to have had a relatively peaceful existence until the 'rough wooing' of 1544. Then Henry VIII, determined to arrange a marriage between the infant Queen Mary and his own young son Edward, dispatched an army to Scotland under the Earl of Hertford – an unusual way, one would think, of promoting a suit.

The Borders suffered appallingly at this time, and none of the abbeys recovered from the depredations inflicted on them. For Dryburgh, the fateful date was Friday, 4 November. Seven hundred men under the command of Sir George Bowes and Sir Brian Layton –

... rode into Scotland upon the water of Teide to a town called Dryburgh with an Abbey in the same, which was a pretty town and well buylded; and they burnt the same town and abbey, saving the churche, with a great substance of corne and got very much spoylage ... sixty nagges and a hundred sheip ... and they tarried so long at the burning and spoylage that it was a Satterday at eight of the clokke at nychte or they come home ...

Where a pretty and well built town once stood, there is now no more than a tiny hamlet of cottages.

Ownership of the ruined abbey passed through various hands until it was given to the nation by Lord Glenconner. Among its most colourful proprietors was the eccentric Earl of Buchan, whose idea of the appropriate was so bizarre that he once burst into Walter Scott's sickroom to announce his plans for the great man's funeral. But he built the original suspension bridge at Dryburgh, and expressed his admiration for the Scottish patriot William Wallace by erecting a statue of him in the middle of a wood, about a mile from the abbey. Though somewhat crudely carved in red sandstone by a local mason, it is certainly an arresting sight for those who care to take the path to where it stands. Scott loathed it, and confessed to Hogg that he would willingly have dynamited it. Hogg, on the other hand, rather admired it. Remembering their different characters and backgrounds, one can understand the effect it had on each.

The signposts near Dryburgh all point to Scott's View. From here you can see, as he loved to, the Tweed sweep round in generous curves among wooded hills, with the triple peaks of the Eildon Hills as a backdrop, while on the horizon stretches the panorama of the Cheviots, the Ettrick Hills and the Lammermuirs. So often did he stop his carriage here that on his last journey, to his burial in Dryburgh Abbey, the horses stopped of their own accord at their master's favourite spot. The funeral cortege was a mile long.

The little winding road rejoins the A68 at Leaderfoot, below the towering seventeen-arch viaduct which once carried the railway from Newtown St Boswells. This large modern village straddles the main road about a mile to the south. For a hundred and twenty years its economy depended on its position as a major railway junction, and the withdrawal of that service and the closure of the line hit the village badly. However it is now the administrative capital for the Borders, and the Regional Council headquarters are housed in a modern concrete building once belonging to Roxburgh County Council. Its choice as a centre by the latter may have been as a result of its position on the road and rail networks, but I suspect that its attractions as neutral territory among the competing claims of the proud and jealous burghs weighed even more strongly in its favour.

For farmers as well as administrators, Newtown is an important centre. The auction mart of John Swan and Sons is now the main selling point for livestock, and on market days the village – and the old Railway Hotel – hum with activity as farmers, shepherds and buyers conduct their business.

Another mile to the south is St Boswells, much older and prettier, with a large green which gives the village a pleasant feeling of spaciousness. Like most of the Border villages, St Boswells has a varied social and sporting life; unlike the others, it boasts a cricket team. The sight of leisurely matches on a calm summer evening gives the place a curiously English air. St Boswells is also the home of the kennels of the Buccleuch Hunt, the largest and most prestigious of the several packs of hounds in the area.

St Boswells Fair, held in July, was once a great occasion – an important social and trading gathering, drawing people from all over the Borders, a time for exchange of news and sale of lambs. James Hogg declined an invitation to London for George IV's coronation, as he 'really could not miss Boswells fair'. The fair still exists, but as a meeting point for the modern travelling people. For me, there is little charm in the sight of a fleet of luxurious chromium-plated homes cluttering up St Boswells green; but you can find a genuine gypsy to read your palm if such things appeal to you. Of livestock trading there is no sign.

OPPOSITE *The graceful arches of the disused viaduct over the Tweed at Leaderfoot, near Newtown St Boswells, provide an outstanding example of railway architecture.*

76

SEVEN

KELSO : ARCHITECTURAL RICHES

From St Boswells, with its attractive old cottages, modern bungalows and a few grand mansions, there is a variety of routes to Kelso. Rather than take the road that winds along the main street, and past the old house of Lessudden (the ancient name for the village), I have chosen the one that turns sharp left off the main A68 at the southern end of St Boswells green. This takes us through the village of Maxton, which has declined as St Boswells and Newtown have expanded. In the Middle Ages its population was around five thousand; now it scarcely reaches three figures. From here, in 1545, a gallant lass by the name of Lilliard followed her lover who had answered the call to arms by Scott of Buccleuch and Kerr of Ferniehirst at the time of Hertford's invasion. The Borderers were to aid the Earl of Angus at Ancrum Moor in what turned out to be the last battle between a Scots and an English army. The Scots were victorious, but Lilliard saw her lover slain and rushed into the fray herself. The inscription on her tombstone at Lilliardsedge, the site of the battle, tells the story:

OPPOSITE *Floors Castle, the home of the Duke and Duchess of Roxburghe, 'set in a land fit for Oberon and Titania'.*

> Fair Maiden Lilliard lies underneath this stane,
> Little was her fortune, but muckle was her fame.
> Upon the English loons she laid mony thumps
> And when her legs were cuttit off, she fought upon her stumps.

The road passes through rich farming country, once known as the Granary of Scotland, and the fertile plains here yield rewarding harvests in these days of highly efficient and mechanized farming. The difference between the farmhouses of the valleys, often little more than substantial cottages, and the large and comfortable looking mansions surrounded by mixed and arable farms indicates clearly the difference in income which could always be expected from each.

Kelso itself is a town with much to delight the eye and the imagination. In the last mile or so of the approach to it, there are notable landmarks. On the left, beyond the Tweed, lie the parapets and pepper-pot turrets of Floors Castle, situated, in the words of Sir Walter Scott, 'in a land fit for Oberon and Titania'; and the castle itself looks rather like something from a fairy tale. It was designed by Sir John Vanbrugh – the architect of Blenheim Palace – for the first Duke of

Roxburghe, the ennobled representative of the ancient family of Kerr of Cessford who had, via an earldom, 'wrastled up the Brae' to a dukedom. Remodelled for the sixth Duke in the early nineteenth century by W.H. Playfair, it is the largest inhabited house in Scotland, with a frontage extending to over four hundred feet. It was the setting for the fictional castle in the Tarzan film 'Greystoke'.

Floors opened its doors regularly to the public in 1981, after the accession to the title of the present Duke of Roxburghe. Of especial interest is the furniture of many periods from Germany, Italy and France. There are also fine paintings and tapestries, including one of Floors' greatest treasures, a fifteenth-century Brussels tapestry, collections of exquisite Fabergé boxes and snuff boxes, and fascinating bits and pieces collected by successive Duchesses of Roxburghe. The present young owners have achieved the difficult feat of maintaining a lively family home and a public treasure-house. The stable block is now a splendid tea room; the Floors stud horses are housed on the adjacent farm.

Directly opposite Floors there is a high hump of grass, a deep ditch, and a few unimpressive and crumbling stacks of masonry. That is all that remains of the mighty royal castle at Roxburgh, while of its surrounding burgh there is no trace whatever (the little village of Roxburgh, a few miles away, is not the direct descendant of the vanished burgh). Has any town of similar importance ever been so completely eradicated, other than drowned Atlantis? Here, where the insignificant ruins stand today, was the virtual capital of the ancient kingdom of Northumbria, the fourth most important burgh in Scotland. Here stood one of the cornerstones of the Scottish defence system, rivalling the fortresses of Stirling and Edinburgh in power and strategic importance. Here were streets, houses, churches, and a mint where coins were struck, and here too was one of the favourite residences of Scottish kings in times of peace, the scene of Alexander II's marriage and of his son's birth.

But Roxburgh's strategic importance proved to be its undoing. It was too accessible to invading English armies on their northwards route, and it changed hands frequently. Built to help defend Scotland, it became a base for attacks on her when it fell into English hands. During the wars of independence in the early fourteenth century the castle was captured for Bruce by Sir James Douglas. The story goes that to achieve this he and his men, draped with blankets, crawled on their knees towards the castle under cover of twilight. Nevertheless, it must have been a shortsighted sentry who apparently mistook the creeping figures for cattle. An English soldier's wife was among the first to be surprised by the identity of the attackers, as she crooned to her baby on the parapet:

> Hush, thee, hush, my little pet ye,
> The Black Douglas will not get ye.

– or so we were taught as children.

For a hundred years from the mid-fourteenth century, Roxburgh Castle was

Like the other tributaries of the Tweed, the Teviot provides fine sport for anglers. Here it is seen near its confluence with the Tweed at Kelso.

held by the English. In 1460 James II resolved to retrieve it for Scotland. 'James of the fiery face', as he was called on account of a disfiguring birthmark, was by way of being an amateur expert in the use of cannon and gunpowder, though his interest was to cost him his life. On Sunday, 3 August 1460, he was superintending the discharge towards the castle of a great gun christened 'the Lion'. It exploded, and killed him. Five centuries later, when I fought the by-election for Roxburgh, Selkirk and Peebles I made use of this incident of a big gun misfiring after an ill-judged speech by a prominent Tory who had been brought in as heavy artillery in an effort to retain the seat!

But to return to the past. James's widow, Mary of Guelders, behaved heroically towards her adopted country. She made her way to the Scots camp with her eight-year-old son, and inspired the troops to continue the assault on the castle to a victorious conclusion. Then, recognizing that its existence was a threat to rather than a bastion of Scottish security, she had the hard-won walls demolished. The thoroughness of that work is evident today.

> Fallen are thy towers, and where the palace stood
> In gloomy grandeur waves yon hanging wood;
> Crushed are thy halls, save where the peasant sees
> One moss-clad ruin rise between the trees.

Next to the ruined castle are the grounds of Springwood Park, a mansion built in 1756 and now itself demolished. In its grounds the Border Union Agricultural Society holds an impressive show in July every year, and in September lines of tents, marquees and sheep pens go up again as farmers and shepherds gather for the Kelso Ram Sales, the largest sheep sales in the country. These are the two major annual events at Springwood Park, but other shows, rallies and gatherings also use the grounds as their mecca.

The road into the centre of Kelso crosses the graceful five-span bridge over the Tweed, built in 1800 by the Scots engineer John Rennie. Its design of elliptic arches was used again by him when he came to design Waterloo Bridge in London. The centre of the town is completely unspoiled by modern

A view up the Tweed to Kelso. The town's strategic position has drawn visitors there from the time of the medieval monks, through to its development as a market town, a staging post, and, today, a holiday centre.

additions, and has a remarkably concentrated collection of interesting buildings. Just past the bridge and immediately to the right are the remains of Kelso Abbey. It is the least entire of all the Border abbeys, although once it was the largest and richest of them. The abbot not only presided over the monks – members of the Tironensian order – he also ministered to parishioners in the town. The abbey church had two towers, one of which contained 'many sweet sounding bells', and there were a dozen altars, as well as the high altar, at all of which daily Mass was celebrated. In the adjoining cloister were not only the monks' quarters – chapter-house, dormitory and refectories – but also 'many houses and lodgings; there are also guest quarters common to both Scots and English. There are granaries and other places where merchants and the neighbours store their corn, wares and goods and keep them safe from enemies. There is also an orchard and a beautiful garden ... [the abbey's] value is somewhat uncertain because of the continued raids and pillages of enemies and robbers ...'. The final raid and pillaging, here as in the other abbeys, was by the

Beyond the bridge built by the Scottish engineer James Rennie, the fine buildings of Kelso reflect the best in architectural styles of several generations.

83

Earl of Hertford during the 'rough wooing' of 1545. Monks and townspeople together held out gallantly, making a last stand in the abbey tower, but the English guns proved too much in the end: the tower was taken and its defenders slain.

Opposite the abbey and just past the bridge is the old toll house, and next door a large garage, the headquarters of Messrs Croall, Bryson & Sons. Croall's Coachbuilding Works operated from this site before the advent of the motor car, building carriages for the great, from Queen Victoria downwards. Behind it is Abbey Court, with its Turret House, a charming little close of well-preserved seventeenth-century houses.

But though Kelso brims over with individual treasures, it is the overall impression created by elegant streets radiating from the fine paved square – the largest in Scotland – that delights and surprises. I say surprises because the square has a European rather than a Scottish character: to me it seems to bear an uncanny resemblance to the square at Maastricht in Holland, right down to the architecture of the town hall and its clock tower. In the centre of the square can still be seen the bull ring, where cattle were tethered on market days, for it was as a market town and a trading centre that Kelso achieved its modest prosperity. The street names surrounding the square indicate their former use: Woodmarket, Coalmarket, Horsemarket, while the bridge over the Tweed that brought the traders also brought the stagecoaches on their journeys north and south. The inns and hotels in the centre of Kelso owe their origins to this trade.

Kelso has always had its manufacturing concerns: in the past, the weaving trade, the leather industry, and the manufacture of the traditional blue bonnets. Today there are electronics firms and diverse small industrial concerns such as the successful factory making archers' bows, which exports all over the world. But Kelso was never industrialized by the woollen trade in the same way as many of the other burghs. Their prosperity dates from the nineteenth century, and much of their architecture reflects this. Kelso's heyday happily coincided with an age when styles were more classically beautiful.

One major contributor to the town's rich heritage was James Dickson, the man for whom both the Cross Keys Hotel and Ednam House, 'the loveliest Georgian town house in Scotland' (also now a hotel, and very finely maintained) were built. He must have been a wayward youth: after breaking a lamp on the town well he decided that pressures in Kelso were more than he could handle, and he ran away to London. There he made his fortune so successfully that he was able to commission the building of these two landmarks on his return to his native town in 1761.

In the world of horses, Kelso is an important centre. At Kelso racecourse just outside the town regular horse sales take place, and races are held several times a year. In the spring the hunting fraternity gathers in the grounds of Floors Castle for point-to-points, and for the relatively new sport of team chasing, where a team of riders gallops round a cross-country course. And, in July, the Scottish Horse Driving trials take place in Floors' wonderful setting.

When my constituency included Kelso the town was the last stop on the eve of polling day. Elections in the Borders call for meetings in every village and every town, up to three a night for the whole three weeks' campaign. But the last meeting of all is unlike any other. Since the end of the war, this has by tradition been the Liberal meeting at the Roxy cinema in Kelso, which seats about four hundred. It starts at 10.30 p.m., and Judy and I would drive through the night from Galashiels, listening to the radio reports of the last stages of the election campaign. They invariably included the statement, 'The speeches have all been made; the meetings have all taken place', and we would exclaim, 'Not at the Roxy, they haven't!' The other parties in the Borders have finished their meetings by then, and supporters of all parties crowd into the Roxy stalls and balcony, while a small platform group teeters on chairs in the couple of feet between the screen and the edge of the platform. Heckling at the Roxy is constant and good-humoured, and questions go on until the audience is exhausted – frequently into the small hours of polling day itself. It is always a spirited and climactic end to the long, gruelling weeks of campaigning that precede it.

Kelso has a lively programme of events throughout the year, some of which, such as the Great Tweed Raft Race, attract participants and onlookers from all over Scotland, while others, like the Civic Week in July, are more integral to the ordinary life of the town.

A handsome grey mare waits patiently before going through her paces in the ring at Kelso Horse Sales.

EIGHT

THE CHEVIOT HILLS

From Kelso, as befits a market town, roads radiate in all directions: to Berwick in the east, via three routes; to Selkirk; to Jedburgh and Hawick in the west; northwards to Edinburgh; and south to Newcastle and the Northumberland town of Wooler. It is this last road we now take, deep into the rolling Cheviot Hills which form the central part of the boundary between Scotland and England. This road takes us to the valley of the Bowmont Water which rises, in a series of fan-shaped burns, on the upper slopes of the Cheviots, almost on the border itself. It flows through the Yetholm villages and crosses into England to join the River Till.

There are two villages bearing the name of Yetholm: Town Yetholm and Kirk Yetholm. The latter, the older one, stands at the northernmost end of the Pennine Way, and is popular with hill walkers. Once, though, feared and shunned by outsiders, it was the headquarters of the powerful gypsy clan of Faas, and the domain of the gypsy king and queen. Those who intruded were made unwelcome with 'aik sticks and bull pups'. You can still see traces of gypsy ancestry in the faces of some of the old Yetholm families, and a row of cottages in the village is still called Gypsy Row. But the Faas as a tribe have long since died out.

From Town Yetholm the road follows the Bowmont Water as far as the farm of Primside Mill, then leaves it to join Kale Water a little further on. The peaks of the Cheviots overshadow the way: Staer Rig, Black Hag, Crookside Head, Cock Law, The Schel, Mosie Law, Brownhart Law, and so on – fine-sounding names for peaks that in places rise to over two thousand feet.

The Cheviots have their own breed of hardy hill sheep. They need to be tough for this is a land where a living is wrung from the land only by incessant toil and battle against the elements. In summer it may be mild enough – though the hills often catch the rain – but when the Yetholm shepherds gather at the beginning of October for their annual show, the winter and all it entails is beginning to close in.

The sheep which pass through the marts on their way to city butchers and processing plants, and whose wool trundles off on lorries in all directions, must be tended not only when the summer grass fills their bellies. In difficult and often dangerous conditions their intake must be maintained throughout the winter months, with daily hay and supplementary feeding. Only with careful

OPPOSITE *Between the villages of Yetholm and Morebattle stands Linton Kirk, which dates from 1160. It stands on a hummock of pure sand, the origins of which are obscure.*

The interior of Linton Kirk contains some fine architectural detail, and a Norman font carved from one piece of stone.

RIGHT *In the village of Kirk Yetholm, under the lee of the Cheviots, the houses are only a stone's throw from the border.*

The quaintly named
Teapot Street in
Morebattle contributes to
the village's old-fashioned
atmosphere.

LEFT *This fine upstanding tup, or
ram, is a splendid example of the
hardy sheep bred in the Cheviots.*

winter tending will come the successful lambing on which the hill farmer depends. And that too can be thwarted by a sudden late onslaught of wintry weather.

When the lambing season starts, social life stops for the farmer, his family and his workers. It is round-the-clock activity to which all must turn their hand. Weak lambs must be revived and given extra attention; motherless ones – and the loss of every lamb or ewe is a diminution of actual or projected capital and income – are either bottlefed or fostered to a ewe whose lamb has died. This can be a tricky business, involving the skinning of the dead lamb and the encasing of another in its hide in order to persuade the surrogate mother to accept it. Recently some farmers have adopted a strange looking means of protecting their lambs from the weather. The small white forms sport plastic overcoats of bright blue or red polythene during their early weeks. I am not sure how much of an improvement this is over nature's provisions: I hope it is considerable, for the aesthetic effect is very odd.

That the sheep one sees on the Border hillsides and in the markets are healthy and well covered by firm flesh and luxuriant coats is the result of persistent, skilled work by a hardy breed of men and women. Work is demanding and financial rewards low, but the face of a Border shepherd tells its own tale in the qualities of strength, character and tranquillity displayed there.

A slight detour on the road between Yetholm and the next village, Morebattle, brings us round by Linton Kirk. Its antecendents go back to the twelfth century, and its walls are believed to date from the same period as Kelso Abbey. The porch carvings depict a dragon-slaying scene. Dragons, or worms as they were more prosaically known in the north, were a recurring theme in the mythology of the ancient kingdom of Northumbria. Although prevalent in the folklore south of the border, worms continued to form part of the oral tradition here too for centuries. Linton parish church is beautifully situated on a tumulus: it was around this that the local worm entwined itself until killed, not by a knight or an incipient saint, but by the local blacksmith.

Morebattle is a particularly old-fashioned village, remote under the hills. Judy says that she began to learn what passions could be aroused in Border villages when, just before my adoption as candidate, she was involved in a legal case of disputed land ownership in Morebattle. The piece of ground in question was one foot wide: in vain did the judge call the parties into his chambers in the Court of Session to persuade them of the folly of pursuing a hearing running into thousands of pounds. A matter of principle was involved; a matter of principle had to be settled. All the unfortunate judge did was ensure for himself a stream of angry letters after the case from the unsuccessful pursuer.

A few miles from Morebattle, on the road to Oxnam, stand the remains of Cessford Castle, once the home of the Kerrs of Cessford who emerged, like the Scotts of Buccleuch, as one of the two leading Border families after the power-hungry Douglases fell from grace. The Earl of Surrey, in 1523, reckoned Cessford to be 'the third strongest place in Scotland', and had the Kerr of the

Not only does Carter Bar mark the boundary between Scotland and England, it is also the site of the last major skirmish on the border : the Raid of the Redeswire took place here in 1575.

day not surrendered the castle in a fairly supine fashion, the English commander would have expected its defence to have been successful. Its fourteen-foot walls still stand, a roofless and stark testament to the past.

In the early sixteenth century we find the Kerrs of Cessford and Scotts of Buccleuch locked in an implacable blood-feud; but by the 1570s the representatives of the two houses were together leading the last, hopeless defence of Mary Stuart's cause. That co-operation continued as the bold Buccleuch and Sir William Kerr of Cessford, Wardens of the Marches, endeavoured to keep order in this most wayward of all parts of the kingdom. By the time Buccleuch was raised to the peerage in 1606, the breach had been finally healed by his marriage to a daughter of the Kerr family. It was at this time that the Kerrs adopted the Roxburghe title and, as we have already seen, they eventually abandoned the desolate Cessford for the grandeur and comfort of Floors Castle.

After Oxnam, the small road wends its way towards the A68, the main trunk road between Newcastle and Jedburgh. But before we turn towards Jedburgh, we must first travel south to visit one of the most dramatic of national frontiers. Here at Carter Bar the hills unfold to create a natural divide between north and south; here the returning traveller to either homeland may well think on Scott's lines:

> Breathes there a man with soul so dead
> Who never to himself has said,
> 'This is my own, my native land'?

93

NINE

JEDBURGH

Avisitor approaching Jedburgh from the south receives the full visual impact of the abbey, standing full square on a rise and still sufficiently intact, despite many depredations, to display its fine proportions. So it must have looked to the English invaders who time and again unleashed on Jedburgh, the first settlement north of the border, the main brunt of their attack.

Jedburgh Abbey was originally founded as a priory in 1118 by the then Prince David of Scotland, and raised to abbey status by him as king twenty-nine years later. His endowment of it was generous:

The monastry of Jedworthe, with everything belonging to it; the tithes of the two Jedworths, Langton, Nesbyt and Creling, the town of Earl Gospatric, with the consent of his chaplain: and in the same town, a ploughgate and half and three acres of land, with two houses: also the tithes of the other Creling, the town of Orm, the som of Eylav; and of Scrauseburghe: the chapel situated in the forest opposite Herningslawe: also, Ulfston, near Jedworth: Alneclive, near Alncromb, Crunsethe, and Reperlawe ...

The list goes on. Even in this brief extract, two spellings of a different form of the name of Jedburgh are used, and over the centuries the name appears in documents in no fewer than eighty-three variations. Both Jedburgh's antiquity and its strategic importance account for its frequent appearances in the recorded history of Scotland, the earliest known reference to it being in 854; it claims to be the first established parish in the country. Even today its inhabitants refer to it as Jeddart or Jethart, and the old battle cry of 'Jethart's here!' is incorporated into the town's song:

> Dear Borderland! Nae blench nor fear!
> Dear Borderland! When foe comes near,
> Stand firm and sure, for Jethart's here:
> Stand firm and sure, for Jethart's here!

During the bitter wars of the thirteenth to sixteenth centuries the inhabitants of Jedburgh – monks and townspeople alike – did have to prove that they could stand firm and sure. The town was ravaged constantly, and it is remarkable that either it or the abbey survive at all. At the end of the thirteenth century the

OPPOSITE Jedburgh Jail, now a museum, was built in 1832 in accordance with the more enlightened penal theories of the day. It occupies the site of Jedburgh Castle and looks down on the sensitively restored Canongate.

Evening shadows pattern the long-deserted nave of Jedburgh Abbey. It was originally constructed – from local sandstone – in the twelfth century, but required constant rebuilding over the centuries as a result of despoliation by invading armies.

abbey was so badly damaged that the monks were forced to seek temporary sanctuary in ecclesiastical communities south of the border. Between 1410 and 1464 the town was burned three times; but the restored abbey, to which a few monks had returned, kept going. By 1513, however, the place had again been abandoned, and rather than allow the abbey to decline as a centre of religious life, the townspeople decided to establish an order of medicant Franciscan friars there.

Ten years later came the most savage and sustained attack the town had known. At the command of Henry VIII, the Earl of Surrey stormed into Jedburgh at the head of a vast army. The greatly outnumbered townsfolk held out stoutly, as is evident from Surrey's report to his sovereign: 'I assure your

96

grace that I found the Scots at this time the boldest and hottest that ever I saw in any nation ... Could forty thousand such men be assembled, it would be a dreadful enterprise to withstand them.' But the force of numbers proved irresistible, and Jedburgh was razed to the ground, 'so surely that no garrison or none others shall be lodged there unto the time it be rebuilded.' Still the spirits of its defenders were unbroken: as the victorious English armies slept in their encampments, the horses of Surrey's fellow commander, Lord Dacre, were mysteriously loosened and stampeded into Surrey's lines, with the result that the invading army was eight hundred horses short in the morning. No wonder Surrey's report continued: 'I dare not write the wonders that my Lord Dacre and all his company do say they saw that night six times of spirits and fearful sights. And universally all in their company say plainly the devil was that night among them six times.'

The final pillaging of Jedburgh took place during Henry's 'rough wooing' of the infant Mary Queen of Scots on behalf of his young son Edward in 1544 and 1545. After this, and more so after the Reformation of 1559 had stripped the abbey of its means of support, it decayed into its present condition. Much has been done recently to enhance the abbey and its surroundings: semi-slum properties have been skilfully restored and corrugated iron shacks cleared from the vicinity to allow uninterrupted views of the ruins; and excavations have uncovered the original extent of the abbey premises, and the skeletons of medieval abbots.

Like so many of the Border towns, Jedburgh is a royal burgh. It was also a favourite royal residence: even before the abbey was built a castle had been established there, and it became a regular haunt of the early Scottish kings. It was evidently a special retreat of Alexander III. Here, in 1264, his first wife bore him a son, and twenty-one years later, after the deaths of his wife and son and of all his other children, we find him attending a masque to celebrate his second marriage, in Jedburgh Abbey, to the beautiful young Yolande. At this feast, it is related, a macabre apparition in the form of a skeleton danced in front of the king before wending its way through the ranks of horrified guests. It was regarded as an evil omen, and sure enough, five months later, after hurrying home on a stormy night to his lovely bride,

> Alexander our king was dead
> Whom Scotland led in love and law

and the bitterness of the disputed succession and the struggle for Scotland's independence had begun.

The most famous of Jedburgh's royal connections is with Mary Queen of Scots, who arrived in the town in October 1566 to administer justice to her unruly subjects in the Borders. This was at the time when her star was in the ascendant: she had successfully crushed two risings against her authority; and she had provided Scotland – and indeed England – with an heir, the infant prince James. Her control of the kingdom was as established as it would ever be,

A stretch of arable land near Jedburgh, with Dod Hill in the distance, and the hay harvest awaiting collection.

RIGHT *Until the bales are under cover, the farmer is at the mercy of the weather.*

and the turmoil on the border was less a display of insurrection against the Crown than part of the general way of life of the inhabitants.

Despite many complaints of lawlessness, few cases were presented to the Queen for adjudication, and the offenders who appeared before her were treated mercifully. A letter from a member of her court to Lord Cecil, Queen Elizabeth's Secretary of State grumbled: 'She has not executed one, but has put all offenders to fine.'

It was at Jedburgh, after her ride to Hermitage Castle to visit her wounded lieutenant, Lord Bothwell, that the Queen lay at death's door for nine days, and only through the skill and unconventional treatment of her surgeon, Arnault, did she recover. Her half-brother, the Earl of Moray, meanwhile, always hopeful of achieving the supreme power which his bastard birth denied him, had taken custody of her jewels, as a token, perhaps, of greater rewards that he hoped would follow. In later years, imprisoned, humiliated, and subject to crippling rheumatism, Queen Mary regretted her surgeon's skill: 'Would that I had died at Jedworth!' she mourned; and indeed from this point on her star declined.

It was her son James's rigorous suppression of border feuding that gave rise to the phrase 'Jeddart Justice': hang first and try later. Following the Union of the Crowns, a commission had been set up in 1605 to try to succeed where previous generations had failed. James did not take the same personal charge of affairs that his grandfather, James v, had done – it was his lieutenant, the Earl of Dunbar, who was the actual instigator of the summary proceedings – but James's concurrence can be seen from the indemnity he gave to Sir William Cranstoun. Sir William was employed, with a troop of horsemen, to scour the countryside for malefactors and when, in pursuit of this end, he was required 'oftentimes summarily to make a quick despatch of a great many notable and notorious thieves and villains by putting them to present death without preceding trial of jury or assise or pronunciation of any conviction or doom', the King declared him to have done most dutifully, and exonerated him from all accusations and proceedings in respect of his acts.

I must admit to a particular partiality for Jedburgh. Because of its history as the most prominent seat of justice in the Borders, and its position as the old county town of Roxburghshire, it was until recently the scene of the count for parliamentary elections, and it was from the steps of the town hall, with the beautiful ruined abbey forming a background to the jubilant crowds, that I was first declared 'duly elected to serve as Member of Parliament'.

In those days Jedburgh had the air of a small, derelict industrial town. Its major employer, a rayon factory, had ceased production, and government grants for new industry were not yet available in this part of Scotland. It would have been easy for despondency to settle over the burgh. That it is today a bustling, colourful place is a tribute to the enterprise and imagination of the local authorities over the years. Once the shock of the closure of the rayon works had been digested, the provost of the time set off for the USA, and, painting a highly favourable picture of the industrial benefits of the area, brought back with him a commitment from the first of the American companies to set up production in the Borders: the L.S. Starrett Company, manufacturers of precision tools.

One of my early campaigns was for a bypass to take the stream of traffic that used to wend its way through the town. This new road has freed the centre of Jedburgh for the wonderful redevelopment of the town centre. The sympathy and imagination shown by the architects of the new schemes have earned them European as well as national heritage awards. Each close and alley leads to another discovery; each archway frames another harmonious group of buildings; each new balustrade and window marries the past and the present.

But there are two buildings, apart from the abbey, of especial interest. The house where the ill-fated Queen Mary stayed in 1566 is what is known as a bastel house – a small, solid, semi-fortified building rather larger than a peel tower. It belonged to the great family of the Kerrs of Ferniehirst, which accounts for one of its most interesting features. Its staircase, above the first floor, curves downwards to the right, leaving the impression that something indefinable is amiss. Normally a spiral staircase curves downwards in the other direction, so that a descending defender may steady himself on the central column, and leave his sword arm free to deal with an attacker. But the Kerrs of Ferniehirst had a pronounced family tendency to left-handedness: hence the expression 'kerry-fisted' even today, and hence the existence of this staircase, and a similar one at Ferniehirst Castle (soon to be opened to the public) just outside the town.

The house has every potential in terms of historical and architectural interest, and the Roxburgh Museums Service has exciting plans for its future as a heritage centre devoted to the life of Mary Queen of Scots. Until now, however, the display it has housed, relating both to Queen Mary and the town, has been disappointing: a random mishmash of questionable relics, including a lurid deathmask of the Queen, and a watch which miraculously reappeared, along with a spur, from the bog in which her horse was mired four hundred years earlier. A bemused American visitor asked the attendant on my last visit, 'But how did they know it was hers?', and was told firmly, 'She said she'd lost it there', somehow suggesting that the deceased Queen had confided all this to the custodian only the week before. The historic relics of the town have not been presented coherently, and offerings from admirers of Mary – one wall taken up with violently coloured embroideries of scenes from her life – appear to have been accepted and displayed indiscriminately.

To see Jedburgh's historic attractions, and to see what can be achieved in creating a fascinating small museum, it is not necessary to go far. Jedburgh Jail lies on the site of the old castle at the top of Canongate. It calls itself 'A Georgian Reform Prison', and its contents and reconstructions are fascinating.

From Jedburgh we turn south again, and although our route through the village of Bonchester Bridge is not the one Queen Mary took over four hundred years ago, our destination is the same.

Peniel Heugh monument near Jedburgh was built to commemorate the Battle of Waterloo, and the surrounding woods are planted to resemble the armies' formations at the start of the battle.

LEFT *'Queen Mary's House', which belonged to the Kerrs of Ferniehirst. It was here that Mary Queen of Scots stayed in 1566.*

TEN

LIDDESDALE AND TEVIOTDALE

Queen Mary's ride to Hermitage Castle in 1566 is often called 'the most romantic ride in history', yet it seems highly unlikely that there was anything romantic about it. The expedition was, however, undertaken by one of the most romantic monarchs of all time, over some of the wildest and most beautiful terrain to be found anywhere, and Queen Mary's purpose in undertaking the day's ride of between fifty and sixty miles was to visit the man who became her third husband – James Hepburn, fourth Earl of Bothwell.

It is, of course, their subsequent marriage which has fired the imaginations of countless historical novelists and endowed the ride with romantic overtones; that, coupled with the Queen's near-fatal illness on her return to Jedburgh. But the fact is that there was no contemporary evidence that the visit, to her principal adviser and executive in the region, was prompted by other than political and administrative needs. She had heard on her way south, through Melrose and the other Border towns, that Bothwell had been wounded: he had been involved in an affray with a particularly troublesome reiver, Jock Elliott. The Queen continued her progress to Jedburgh, transacted her business in the town, and then, not unnaturally, visited her Lieutenant to discuss the state of affairs on the border. Her escort included her half-brother Moray and other members of her privy council, a fact which conflicts with the later description of the episode by her biographer and traducer George Buchanan: 'Her affection, impatient of delay, could not temper itself, but she must needs display her outrageous lust, and in an inconvenient time of year, she betook herself headlong into her journey with such a company as no man of any honest degree would have adventured his life and his goods amongst them.' Twentieth-century political commentators have a lot to learn from the sixteenth century when it comes to biased and mendacious reporting!

OPPOSITE *Billihope Hill, near Hermitage Castle.*

Hermitage is not what anyone would describe as a romantic castle. It needs to be seen on a sombre, overcast day – the sun becomes it less well than a shroud of mist. It is a military fortress, evoking no thoughts of masques, minstrels or revelries, only the grim unending struggle to keep the border intact and to achieve some kind of order among the clans. The legends of Hermitage are not tales of chivalry but of cruelty and savagery.

The castle was built in the thirteenth century by the de Soulis family. An early owner, Nicholas de Soulis, was a villainous character, so depraved that the

103

Young conifers cover the hills and valleys of Wauchope Forest.

RIGHT *Ewes and young lambs enjoying early spring sunshine near Newcastleton.*

details of his atrocities have never been revealed. Eventually his despairing vassals took their complaints to the King. 'Oh, *boil* him for all I care,' the King reputedly exclaimed, 'but bother me no longer.' They took him at his word, seized Lord Soulis, and then:

> They wrapped him up in a sheet of lead,
> A sheet of lead for a funeral pall;
> They plunged him in the cauldron red
> And melted him – lead, bones and all.

Later the castle passed into the hands of the great and power-hungry Douglas family. In 1342 Sir William Douglas, known as the Knight of Liddesdale or the Flower of Chivalry, was deprived of the office of Lieutenant of the Border in favour of Sir Alexander Ramsay. Douglas's retribution was slow and terrible, and stripped him forever in the eyes of posterity of his reputation for chivalry. He imprisoned Ramsay in an oubliette in Hermitage and starved him to death.

The fortress, with its blood-stained history, then passed through a succession of families, falling from time to time into the hands of the English. In 1508 Adam Hepburn, Earl of Bothwell, was granted the Lordship of Liddesdale, and with it Hermitage, 'Cum caustro, fortalico, et manerie' ('With castle, fortress and manors'). He was the grandfather of James Hepburn, Mary's Bothwell. The report of the Royal Commission on Ancient Monuments for Roxburgh, published in 1956, slips easily into referring to this fourth Earl of Bothwell as 'notorious'. It was his misfortune that he ended up on the losing side, but his detractors, led by the redoubtable Buchanan, held sway until this century, when more objective assessments of his life and character have redressed the balance.

That he was enigmatic compared with his more self-seeking contemporaries is certain. Born of a father whose treachery both to his wife and his sovereign was unrivalled even in those days, he himself showed an unswerving loyalty to the Queen Regent, Mary of Guise, and to the Queen herself. Nor was that loyalty occasioned by religion, for he embraced Protestantism, though not, apparently, dogmatically. His exploits in pursuit of both Queens' interests were in the Border tradition. His lightning raid in Northumberland, routing an English force under Lord Percy; his capture of gold sent by Queen Elizabeth to aid the rebel lords against the Queen Mother (an action for which neither Elizabeth nor the Protestant lords ever really forgave him); his escape from Holyrood after the murder of Rizzio and his engineering of the Queen's escape – all these adventures would have placed him in a different league from the other sinister plotters who surrounded the Queen had he not made two dreadful errors of judgement. The first – his complicity in the murder of Darnley – he might have lived down (after all, most of his peers were also involved); but his fatal, irremediable mistake was his marriage to the Queen. And that was probably a political act rather than a love match. Bothwell's first marriage was undoubtedly one of expediency, and it is likely that his second was as well. In any event, the union brought both partners inexorably towards defeat, exile, imprisonment and death, she at the hands of her cousin Queen Elizabeth, he after rotting away physically and mentally in a Danish dungeon, where he died insane.

The road leads south from Hermitage to the village of Newcastleton, which was laid out and built by the third Duke of Buccleuch in 1793. It was conceived as a weavers' village, and the holdings were let out on ninety-nine year leases, or tacks. Later, the economy of the village depended heavily on the railway line, and the withdrawal of the service through the Borders in 1969 affected Newcastleton badly. As a last gesture of defiance, when the final passenger train – a night sleeper from Edinburgh to London – was due to pass through, the villagers, headed by the local minister, closed the level crossing gates and stood between them. I was a passenger on the train, and it fell to my lot to persuade the gallant band of demonstrators to disperse, after obtaining an assurance from the police that no charges would be made against the minister, who had by this time been taken into custody.

To come from the sweeping Liddesdale hills into Newcastleton's long and often deserted main street, with its air of expectancy, is strangely evocative of the Wild West. But once a year in early July the town is thronged with people as one of the most popular folk music festivals in Scotland takes place there. The Holm Show at the end of August attracts farmers from all over the region ('Holm' is short for the village's old name of Copshawholm).

My route now enters Dumfriesshire, joining the A7 north of Langholm. At Mosspaul it re-enters the Borders Region, at the old coaching inn which must in the past have proved a welcome sight to travellers along the lonely miles of Teviotdale. Every May the inn receives a sudden invasion, when, as part of the build-up to the Common Riding, the Hawick Cornet at the head of his 'male equestrian supporters' covers the gruelling twenty-five miles from Hawick to Mosspaul and back. It is a punishing journey, over steep hills, swampy passes and unexpected ditches, riding in the footsteps of the old mosstroopers. Those who survive the ride, and the hospitality of the Mosspaul Inn, are admitted to the ancient order of Mosstroopers.

North of Mosspaul, by Teviothead, is a landmark famous in Border balladry. The Armstrongs, along with the Elliots, were among the most lawless of all the Border families: 'Armstrongs and Elliots ride thieves all' was the saying, and Johnnie Armstrong of Gilnockie was, in the mid-sixteenth century, the uncrowned king of Teviotdale. His power and wealth, unethically acquired, were a red rag to James V, who was trying to pacify the unruly Borders – an unceasing preoccupation of the Stuart kings. James's initial overture to Armstrong may have been well meant:

> The King he writes a loving letter
>   With his ain hand sae tenderly,
> And he has sent it to Johnie Armstrong
>   To come and speak with him speedily

The spacious squares and wide streets of Newcastleton are testimony to the fact that the village was planned in its entirety. A memorial to the men of Liddesdale who died in the First War dominates the centre of the village.

although, since he came hot-foot from hanging Cockburn of Henderland in Yarrow, and Adam Scott of Tushielaw in Ettrick, his motives might well have been suspect. The appointed meeting place was Carlinrig, and it was here that the undiplomatic Armstrong flaunted his power before the King:

> When Johnie came before the king
>   Wi' al his men sae brave to see,
> The king he movit his bonnet to him
>   He weened he was a king as well as he.

But the reiver had overplayed his hand. The King seized him, and summarily executed him, though not before Armstrong had fired his immortal parting shot:

> 'Ye lied, ye lied, now king,'
>   'Although a king and prince ye be!
> For I've loved nothing in my life,
>   I weel dare say it, but honesty –
>
> To seek hot water beneath cold ice
>   Surely it is a great folly –
> I have asked grace from a graceless face,
>   But there is none for my men and me.

John was murdered at Carlinrig
And all his gallant company;
But Scotland's heart was ne'er sae wae
To see so many brave men die.

Near Hawick stand the remains of Branxholm Castle, once the seat of the greatest of all the Border families, the Scotts of Buccleuch. They received it for their loyalty to James II in face of an ever-present threat from the Douglases. Here lived the 'wizard lady of Branxholm', Janet Beaton, the middle-aged lover of the young Earl of Bothwell. Four times married, Janet bore six children to Walter Scott of Buccleuch, her third husband, and seems to have loved him dearly. When he was murdered in 1552, by a party of the Kerrs of Cessford in settlement of a long-standing grudge, she was angry that his murderers were sentenced only to banishment for their crime. Mustering two hundred horsemen, she rode at their head in pursuit of a supporter of the Kerrs. He took refuge in the church of St Mary's of the Lowes, but Janet defied the laws of sanctuary, broke down the door with an axe, and wreaked her own vengeance on the fugitive.

It was a Scott of Buccleuch who, along with Kerr of Ferniehirst, was one of the last of the Scots nobles to hold out in defence of Mary Queen of Scots, even after her flight to England and her imprisonment there. As retribution, the supporters of the infant king burned Branxholm Castle. It was completely rebuilt after 1570, and from here the 'Bold Buccleuch', hero of so many ballads, administered the Borders – both according to the book and, when rules were unsatisfactory, in his own spontaneous fashion.

History relates that towards the end of Queen Elizabeth's reign, Buccleuch was admitted to her presence. Referring to his daring rescue of Kinmont Willie from Carlisle Castle, an episode which had enraged her, the English Queen is reputed to have demanded of him, 'How *dared* ye commit so presumptuous an offence?' His reply was in keeping with his character: '*Dare*, madam? What is there that a man dares *not* do?' Elizabeth was not offended: she recognized the great spirit of the man, and observed 'with ten thousand such men, our brother in Scotland might shake the firmest throne in Europe.'

And James did indeed recognize the virtues of his great lieutenant. When, after the Union of the Crowns, he raised the Bold Buccleuch to the peerage, it was with this eulogy: 'For his stout and doughty exertions, to the singular commendation, benefit and praise of the king, and the kingdom and community; and his many and singular abilities, joined with ready and frank inclination and willingness to the king's service, and love to his native country, its interests and honour.'

The character and adventurousness of the clans of Liddesdale and Teviotdale are apparent throughout this century: it was a Scott who died so heroically at the South Pole, an Armstrong who took the 'first small step for man' on the moon.

Carewoodrig Burn, a tributary of Liddel Water.

LEFT *The forbidding walls of Hermitage Castle, to which Queen Mary rode in 1566 to visit the wounded Earl of Bothwell.*

ELEVEN

HAWICK: 'THE AULD GREY TOUN'

The approach to Hawick down Teviotdale (and it is the most attractive way into the town) passes the delightful gardens and museum of Wilton Lodge Park, housing the Borders' best municipal art gallery; they are accessible by footbridge across the river. Ahead are the rugby grounds of Hawick High School, on which so many heroes of that sport have learnt the game, graduating to play for Hawick at Mansfield Park in the famous green jerseys, and for Scotland, at home and abroad. Their excellence is one of Hawick's greatest claims to fame.

Another is its woollens. From the knitwear mills of Hawick come the world-famous names of Pringle, Braemar, Peter Scott, Lyle and Scott, and Barrie.

Hawick is known as 'the Auld Grey Toun', and not even the most fervent Teri could claim that, architecturally, it is other than uncompromisingly industrial. A Teri, I should explain, is a native of Hawick, taking the name from a corruption of the burgh motto: Tyr-Ibus ye Tyr ye Odin. This is so ancient that it defies precise translation, although it is generally believed to be a call for assistance on the old Norse gods, Thor and Odin.

Hawick's antiquity also gives rise to divisions of opinion as to the derivation of the town's name. There are three schools of thought: that its origin is Old English, Celtic, or Latin. Whatever the truth, there were many early variations of the name. 'Hawic' first appears in records in the 1160s, and became a burgh in 1511. However, it remained a small settlement until the founding of the hosiery industry at the end of the eighteenth century. Over the next hundred years the industry and the town expanded together, and now Hawick supplies markets all over the world – a far cry from the original cottage industry of stocking making. The first frames for making men's stockings in Scotland were introduced into Hawick by Bailie John Hardie in 1771. By 1816 the town had over 500 knitting frames turning out over 320,000 pairs. This number grew within a few years to 1,200 frames, and the town's population grew as production increased. In 1801, the population of Hawick stood at under 3,000; by 1838 it had doubled, and by the end of the century the town had reached its peak of population at nearly 20,000.

Throughout the nineteenth century Hawick was at the forefront of the struggle for parliamentary reform. The reform movement had considerable

OPPOSITE St Mary's, the parish church of Hawick, has recently been returned to its position of dominance in the town by the award-winning scheme for clearing and renovating adjacent decaying properties.

support in all the Border towns, but Hawick was the main focus of political activity. Nor is that surprising: before 1830, out of a population of around five thousand, there were precisely three parliamentary voters in the town! The support for the Reform Bill was led by the magistrates, who convened a public meeting which passed the resolution that 'a full, free, and equitable representation in the Commons House of Parliament is the undoubted right of every British subject.'

At the election of 1831 a contingent marched on polling day from Hawick to Jedburgh, in support of the Liberal candidate, William Elliot of Stobs. Although defeated, he was adjudged the moral victor, and it was he, and not the winning Tory, who was carried shoulder-high around the town. A hundred and thirty years later, after the by-election, I too was hoisted on to shoulders and carried round the streets of Jedburgh. And the songs that my supporters were singing so lustily were the Hawick songs!

When the Reform Act of 1832 was eventually passed by the recalcitrant House of Lords, the number of voters in Hawick increased to 346. The magistrates celebrated in style. An open-air dinner was arranged on the common ground known as the Haugh, and the procession beforehand, with well over a thousand men led by three bands, was reckoned to be the most spectacular event the town had ever seen.

Hawick continued to be a centre in the struggle for universal male suffrage throughout the century. To counteract the Liberal ascendancy in the Borders, Tory sympathizers from outside the area bought parcels or 'faggots' of land in the constituency in order to qualify for a vote. It was a flagrant abuse of the electoral system and aroused tremendous hostility. We have already seen the riots which this practice caused in Peebles: in Hawick opposition to such injustice reached its peak, as Edinburgh residents arriving to cast their vote were unceremoniously bundled out of their carriages and dumped in the River Teviot. One writer, describing political events in Hawick at the time, confessed that as a child he had not realized that the Tories were actually human beings, of the same form and substance as himself. In such terms were they described that he thought their place was in demonology.

In the Wilton Lodge Museum, which houses an interesting collection showing the development of the hosiery industry, there is a relic of Hawick's nineteenth-century radical past displayed. A banner, carried during the demonstrations in favour of the Chartist Movement, bears the following adaptation of Robert Burns' great poem on brotherhood:

> Though Salisbury say nae vote ye'll hae,
>   It's coming yet for a' that,
> When ilka man throughout the land
>   Shall hae a vote, an' a' that.

The Reform Act of 1868 gave the vote to all male householders in the burgh constituencies. After much consultation and discussion with the townspeople

of Hawick and Galashiels, it was decided that these towns, together with Selkirk, should be formed into one seat known as the Border Burghs, or the Hawick Burghs. Though every male householder now had the vote in the burghs, this was not the case in the country seats, however, where the franchise was still limited.

The radical Liberal George Trevelyan held the Border Burghs seat until 1886; for the first few elections he was unopposed. He held many government offices, including that of Secretary of State for Scotland. During that time the pressure continued for complete male suffrage, with the Borders the scene of many a mass meeting. The largest of these took place in Hawick in September 1884: trains brought demonstrators from Galashiels and the other towns, and the meeting topped 10,000 – half the size of the town's total population.

Trevelyan fell out with Gladstone over Irish Home Rule, and in 1886 was opposed not by a Conservative but by a Home Rule Liberal, A.L. Brown, a Galashiels tweed manufacturer. When I first came to Ettrick Bridge, I was introduced to a frail old lady in her nineties. 'I wish you success', she said, 'My brother Sandy won the Border Burghs for Mr Gladstone in 1886.'

The Border Burghs seat was amalgamated into Roxburgh and Selkirk in 1918. There is no evidence that I know of that much support was given to the women's suffrage movement, an omission that would surprise no-one who knows Hawick. It is no place for feminists. The attributes which produced the sturdy front-line troops who defended Scotland's boundary and identity, which sent men demonstrating and battling and rejoicing in the fight to establish democracy, are to be found in the rugby footballers of Hawick today. The town has often justified its self-appointed title as leader in the field of Scottish rugby:

> What though her lads are wild a wee,
>   And ill tae keep in order,
> 'Mang ither toons she bears the gree,
>   Hawick's Queen o' a' the Border.

The concentrated passion for the sport does have its parallels, chiefly in the Welsh valleys, where the miners devote themselves to the game with as much religious fervour as do the Hawick millworkers. But it is the scale of the Borders' contribution in relation to the size of the region which is amazing. The entire population of the Borders (including Berwickshire, which has no first-division clubs) is just under 100,000. Yet from this number there regularly comes a high proportion of the Scottish team. In 1984, of the magnificent Scottish team who brought home the Calcutta Cup, the Triple Crown and the Championship, over two thirds were from the Borders.

Hawick's recent hero, the yachtsman Chay Blyth, exemplifies again the spirit of rugged independence and self-sufficiency that has filtered down the generations. When, in 1973, the Town Council of Hawick honoured Chay with the freedom of the burgh, the occasion was charged with emotion. The young man had actually done what some of his elders and contemporaries had dreamed of, but never achieved.

The masculine traditions of the town show themselves again in the Hawick Common Riding which takes place at the beginning of June. In the weeks preceding the main celebrations, the Cornet leads 'ride-outs' to villages and places of historic interest in the surrounding district. The most prestigious and toughest of these is, as I have already described, the one to Mosspaul. They follow a set timetable from year to year; nevertheless the Cornet duly advertises each week an invitation for his 'male equestrian supporters' to follow him, and this last bastion of male supremacy has remained unbreached. In the 1950s some plotters from Galashiels persuaded a girl to disguise her identity and follow the Hawick Cornet to Mosspaul. Suspicions were aroused and the girl was unmasked; the incident was not treated as a joke.

'The Cornet and his merry men On mettled steeds are prancing.'

Enthusiastic callants fulfil the words of the Hawick song as they follow the cornet on the arduous ride to Mosspaul.

The bracken-covered slopes of White Hill, near Hawick.

OPPOSITE *Easter Park Hill above Borthwick Water, three miles west of Hawick.*

Hawick Common Riding has a special character. At the sight of the men of the town riding out behind their top-hatted, green frock-coated Cornet, the centuries roll back. The majority ride on rough, shaggy beasts, and it is only the younger followers who wear the precautionary headgear: for the most part they go bareheaded. There is a particular Hawick seat on a horse, with stirrups shorter than any riding school will teach.

The Cornet, chosen by his predecessors to lead the town's festivities, represents the young unmarried men, or 'callants' of centuries past. In the dismal days of 1514, the year after Flodden, when the men of the town had been decimated in battle, the callants kept the defence of Hawick and won a minor but memorable skirmish at Hornshole, near the town. So by tradition, the Cornet must be unmarried (an 'Acting Father' represents the town's married men); he must also undertake to remain so during the two subsequent years

116

when he will act as supporter to his successor. It is a hard burden to place on a man in his early twenties, and on his girlfriend, but the honour of being Cornet, and Cornet's Lass, is reckoned to be full compensation for a postponed marriage.

And even if tradition bars 'Hawick's bright-eyed daughters' from participating in the Common Riding on horseback, the Cornet's Lass plays a major role in the pageantry. On the Thursday of Common Riding week, 'The Nicht afore the Morn', the ceremony of Bussing the Colours takes place in the town hall, when the Cornet's Lass, clad like her twenty-four maids of honour in a picture hat and a long dress, ties ribbons on to the burgh flag carried by the Cornet. It is a picturesque tradition, and though the flag is 'bussed' in other towns too, greater prominence is given to the ceremony in Hawick than elsewhere. It must have evolved from the days when warriors carried a lady's favour into tournament or battle. The Cornet is preceded into the packed hall by the evocative sound of the Fife and Drum band – one of the few of its kind remaining – whose rendering of the old Hawick song is taken up by the informal male chorus that packs the gallery:

> Teribus ye teri odin,
> Sons of heroes slain at Flodden,
> Imitating Border bowmen
> Aye defend your rights and common!

This is the curtain-raiser to the Common Riding weekend of celebrations in early June.

Hawick is a close-knit town; even its accent is distinctive. It is sometimes called the 'yow and mei' dialect (the Hawick equivalent of 'you and me'). The traditions of the town are guarded by the influential Callants Club, which was founded at the beginning of the century. The War Office had bought the nearby estate of Stobs, and it was believed that a large-scale army camp would be set up there. A group of Teris mostly connected with the Common Riding founded the club to preserve the customs of the town against the expected influx of outsiders. In the event, Stobs was used only as a minor camp, and for internment of German prisoners, but the Callants Club flourished and continues to uphold the history and traditions of the town. The 'Horse', that poignant statue of a mounted bygone callant bearing a pennant, which dominates one end of the High Street, was provided by the Club.

Before leaving Hawick, let us take a look at the processes involved in producing the woollen garments for which the town is famous. An important feature of the industry is that only the highest grades of wool are used – cashmere accounts for a large proportion of the production – and all the garments are fully fashioned: Hawick knitwear goes to the luxury end of the market.

When the yarn arrives from the spinning mills in Galashiels, Selkirk and further afield, it has been spun and dyed but is still very greasy. The first

*'Up wi' the banner high':
this statue, known simply
as 'The Horse' was given
to the town by the Hawick
Callants' Club in 1914.*

production stage is the making up on machines – still known as 'frames' – of the ribs: cuffs, welts, necks and so on. Then the ribs are transferred, stitch by stitch, to the frames where the bodies are fashioned. Technology has greatly increased the amount each worker can handle, but has not dispensed with the necessity for that worker to be skilled with eye and finger. The third stage is the stitching of side and shoulder seams – traditionally a process carried out by women – and the joining of the various components. Then the garments are thoroughly washed in the soft Hawick water to rid the wool of its natural oils. Drying the garment after this, allowing for exactly the correct degree of shrinkage, is another highly skilled part of the process. In the finishing department the final touches are made. Necks are cut and bound, buttons attached, and the garments go for a final press and check before making their way, via the despatch area, to destinations all over the world.

TWELVE

A CLUSTER OF VILLAGES

The hinterland between the two main trunk routes in the central Borders – the A7 and the A68 – contains a cluster of pleasant villages. They have various individual attractions, and also a common core of activities. I am always aware that in describing villages and towns as 'large' and 'small' I do so in terms of the Borders. In the south of England a community of five thousand would probably be described as a village: here it is a medium-sized town. And Galashiels and Hawick, large towns by my definition, both have under twenty thousand inhabitants. A 'big village' here has perhaps five hundred souls.

I think it is fair to say that nothing arouses greater passion in the villages than its school. It is a symbol of vitality or decay; when it goes, the heart is considered to leave the community, and the loss of the school will make not only the village but the surrounding farms less attractive to families with young children. A community with a school, a church, a shop and a pub is always seething with the small-scale but intense politics which they generate. The appointment of a new teacher, the sale of the schoolhouse, the linking of the parish with its neighbour and the sharing of a minister, the change in ownership of a pub or the retirement of a shopkeeper – all these events cause tidal waves rather than ripples in the village concerned.

In the larger villages, such as Denholm or Lilliesleaf, a sawmill or a small joinery or building firm often provides a few jobs for local people, and the traditional skills of dyking, fencing or blacksmithing (the latter usually includes an agricultural engineering service nowadays) occupy some more. The hotels and pubs are generally family concerns, offering part-time employment rather than a living to those outside the family. Modern craftsmen with a liking for rural life have been drawn here from outside the region, and every village now seems to have its pottery; small art galleries abound, and cottage industries of glassware, woodturning, furniture making and other such skills all manage to provide a reasonable level of income.

On this roundabout route between Hawick and Melrose, Denholm is the first village we come to. It lies within the parish of Cavers, the last lands of the once mighty Black Douglas family. Cavers is dotted with the sites of ancient earthworks and forts, the most substantial of which is the Roman Signal Station on Rubers Law. What a vantage point this must have been, situated on one of the most conspicuous of all the Border landmarks.

OPPOSITE *Bowden Kirk stands just outside the village of that name. Both Bowden and the neighbouring village of Midlem are conservation areas.*

The church at Cavers predates the one at Denholm, which was formerly the United Free Church. In fact there are two churches to be seen here: the gracious late Georgian building, still more popular with many of the inhabitants of Denholm than their own village church, and its abandoned predecessor, parts of which date from seven hundred years ago. Bishop Turnbull, distinguished founder of Glasgow University, was born in the neighbouring parish of Bedrule.

Denholm village itself, once famous for stocking weaving, is still clustered round a spacious green, which actually comprises four different areas: the Large Green, the Small Green, the Quoiting Green and the Bleaching Green. On the southernmost corner of the village is Westgate Hall, a particularly good and rare example of a middle-class Scottish house of the seventeenth century. At the opposite corner is a row of thatched cottages, one of which was the birthplace of Denholm's local hero, John Leyden. Leyden was yet another friend and contemporary of Scott's. Like Hogg, he was the son of a shepherd, but unlike the Ettrick poet he achieved – and achieved is a more appropriate word then received – an education. He was an intellectual whose academic success was attained in the face of enormous odds. From an early age he showed unusual brilliance at local schools, and in 1790, at the age of fifteen, he set off for Edinburgh University, walking all the way from Galashiels. He studied for the ministry – a safe profession for a brilliant youth of humble background – but made no headway in that line. His voice – 'like a parrot' – could scarcely have been a help.

Leyden was instrumental in helping Scott collect the old ballads for the *Minstrelsy*, and contributed some of his own verse. His scholarliness is said to have restrained Scott's more gothic flights of fancy in repairing the fragmented ballads, and ensuring their simple purity. Meanwhile he was discovering his true propensity – a remarkable flair for languages combined with a yearning for travel. However much he was at home in his native valleys, he yearned for the East. Despite his amazing repertoire of languages (by the time he died he had mastered no less than forty-five), the only openings he could find were for surgeons. So he set himself to qualify in that profession as well, still finding time to write his collection of poems about the landscape of the Jed and Teviot, *Scenes of Infancy*.

In 1803 Leyden achieved his ambition of a post in India. In time, he became Professor of Hindustani in Calcutta, and a judge in the High Court there. His success was aided by the Governor of the time, the Earl of Minto. The Minto family estate adjoins Denholm village, and the Governor naturally took an interest in the advancement of a prodigy from his own neighbourhood. Leyden never returned to Scotland; eight years after he had left his native land he died of fever in Java.

Leyden was not the only literary figure to emerge from Denholm: it also claims as one of its sons the first editor of the Oxford English Dictionary, James Murray.

122

A First World War soldier stands beside the battlemented tower of Minto Church.

The churchyard in the village of Minto, near Denholm, deserves a visit on account of its remarkable memorial to the First World War. It is the work of Thomas Clapperton, a fine sculptor whose statues can be seen in several Border towns. His figure of a weary soldier, forever on guard in the quiet of Minto churchyard, has one of the strongest emotional impacts of all the monuments raised to that awful carnage.

Like Denholm, the village of Ancrum has its village green, until recently adorned with ancient trees. Constant battles have raged in the local papers between the more vocal inhabitants of Ancrum and the district council, whose policy of pruning, lopping, and eventually felling these trees has come under

Two aspects of the small-scale economy which thrives on the Borders' large horse population: FAR LEFT Jim Scott, one of the area's most experienced blacksmiths in his forge at Midlem, and LEFT Robert McNab, who runs a flourishing saddlery business from Darnick.

123

fire. But the new-look green, with its young trees, is actually an improvement on the rather sombre, overshadowed aspect which it used to wear, and for the first time in many years the fine old market-cross is clearly visible.

Not far from Ancrum, on the other side of the A68, is Monteviot House, the home of the Marquis of Lothian, head of the ancient family of Kerr of Ferniehirst. The Liberal predecessor of the present holder of the title was the distinguished diplomat Lord Lothian, the British Ambassador to Washington during the war years. The present Lord Lothian was a minister in Edward Heath's government, and his heir, the Earl of Ancram, now sits in the House of Commons as a Conservative MP for Edinburgh South.

Lothian Estates have developed an interesting Woodland Centre at Monteviot. It is partly educational, in its exposition of the processes of the timber industry, and partly recreational, in its provision of signposted woodland walks. Its commercial side is taken care of by the sale of young trees from the estate nursery, and by the consortium of craftsmen working in wood, who operate from the workshops at the centre.

After this excursion across the trunk road, I return to Ancrum, and thence to Lilliesleaf, a quiet village with an uneventful history. Like Ancrum and Denholm, Lilliesleaf has its own version of the 'Handba' game', usually associated with Jedburgh. It is a game with no apparent rules, played on set dates in the year, when the local lads, divided into teams of 'Uppies' and 'Doonies' battle to pass a ball over a 'Haling line' marking a rough kind of goal at each end of the main street. The ball is supposed to represent the skull of an English soldier.

From Lilliesleaf, with its shops, pubs, school and church, we go through the pretty village of Midlem, which has none of these. Bowden, too, is a quiet place, though larger in size. Its church, a little way out of the village, dates from the seventeenth century (though the foundation of a church on the site dates from six hundred years earlier) and has some good carvings and an interesting laird's loft. The inscription below the loft contains the kind of dour warning that could be expected of those unforgiving times:

> BEHOLD THE AXE LIES AT THE TREES ROOT
> TO HEW DOWN THOSE THAT BRINGS NOT FORTH GOOD FRUIT
> AND WHEN THEY'RE CUT THE LORD INTO HIS IRE
> WILL THEM DESTROY AND CAST INTO THE FIRE.

Clearly the author of these lines did not have much time for the doctrine of the redemption of souls.

Bowden lies nestled below the Eildon Hills, those omnipresent guardians of the Central Borders, visible on the horizon from almost every angle. Throughout the seasons they provide a backcloth of ever-changing light and colour, whether the rich russet of the earth is bare or blanketed in snow, or covered with blazing golden gorse or purple heather. The road from Bowden skirts their lower slopes, and winds down to the lovely small town of Melrose.

The triple peaks of the Eildon Hills, source of much ancient folklore, are a focal landmark from all directions.

LEFT *The Leyden monument in the village of Denholm. The houses surrounding the Green are held by their owners under feudal tenure, and a feuars' council still exists.*

THIRTEEN

MELROSE AND ITS ABBEY

I choose Melrose as the starting point for an examination of the Border abbeys not because it is the oldest of King David's foundations – Kelso claims that distinction – but because the Melrose area is the cradle of Christianity in the Borders. For this reason perhaps, Melrose still has an ecclesiastical air. Jedburgh, to me, is essentially a frontier town; Kelso exudes the atmosphere of a market town; Hawick and Galashiels are uncompromisingly industrial; but in Melrose the ruined abbey is still predominant.

King David's abbey was not the original foundation of Melrose. For that we need to go to a site a few miles up the Tweed, and back in time five centuries from David's day to that of Oswald, King of the ancient kingdom of Northumbria, who reigned between 635 and 642. Previous efforts to bring Christianity to the kingdom had failed: the importation of the southern, Roman, influence of St Augustine touched few chords in the hearts of the Northumbrians. But Oswald looked west, to the Celtic Church of St Columba, and enrolled the energetic Aidan to organize missionary work from the monastery he had founded on the island of Lindisfarne. Under Aidan's direction, missionaries went to all parts of Oswald's realm. One of his lieutenants was Boisil, who followed the Tweed up to the horseshoe bend that we look down on from Scott's View, and on this idyllic spot known as Old Melrose, he founded the monastery of 'Mailros'.

Thus Boisil, whose name is commemorated in the village of St Boswells, was the father of the Christian faith in the Borders. But it was Cuthbert, his successor and protégé, who ranks higher in the calendar of saints of the once-great Celtic Church. Cuthbert was a shepherd boy, whose quiet life in the Border hills seems to have been abruptly altered by an experience strangely parallel to that of the Bethlehem shepherds six and a half centuries before. As his companions slept and Cuthbert kept watch, he saw a vision of the heavens opening and angels descending, 'to receive a spirit of exceeding brightness'. He later learned that the moment of his vision had coincided with the death of the great St Aidan, and this was to change the course of his life. He left his flocks to others and set out for the monastery of Melrose. Here Boisil, the prior, instantly recognized Cuthbert's saintly qualities and greeted him with the words, 'Behold the servant of the Lord'. Boisil took charge of the young man's spiritual progress, and when he died 'of pestilence', Cuthbert succeeded him as prior.

OPPOSITE *'Now Bowden moor the march-man won'. Scenes such as this, near Bowden, form the background to William of Deloraine's ride in 'The Lay of the Last Minstrel'.*

But a contemplative monastic life was not for the Border saint. He was a charismatic and energetic evangelist, who preached the word of God in all the Border villages in a tongue which his hearers could understand, and in terms with which they could identify. According to his biographer, Bede, he was a gifted orator, and had a fine physical presence; moreover, he never lost his simplicity and spirituality. Around Cuthbert, legends grew up in his lifetime, endowing him with mystical and miraculous powers comparable with those of Christ, while his empathy with the animal kingdom seems to have rivalled that of St Francis of Assisi. An eagle is reported to have brought him food for a journey; and there is a stranger legend which involves two otters. Cuthbert had a custom of doing penance by immersing himself up to the neck in water while he prayed. At Coldingham he performed this ritual in the sea: as he emerged, a witness claimed to have seen two otters follow him and dry his cold, wet feet with their breath and rub him with their fur.

From Melrose he went to Lindisfarne as abbot. He retired from there to become a hermit, and finally, reluctantly, he accepted a bishopric at Lindisfarne. The tales of his miraculous influence did not cease at his death, for his earthly remains were imbued with supernatural powers. According to legend, his body was taken on a seven-year journey down the Tweed: all its resting places were accorded special sanctity, and the stone coffin is said to have floated on the water.

The monastery founded by Boisil continued to flourish until the end of the eleventh century, by which time it seems to have fallen into decay and to have been reduced in status to the chapel of St Cuthbert, a mecca for pilgrims. No trace remains of either monastery or chapel at the original site.

When, in 1136, King David – the son of Malcolm Canmore, first ruler of a united Scotland, and his saintly Saxon Queen, Margaret – established the Border abbeys, he chose a new site for the Cistercians of Melrose, and richly endowed their new abbey. Besides the surrounding lands of Melrose, Eildon and Gattonside, and fishing rights in the Tweed, he granted the monks timber and pasturage in the forests of Selkirk and as far away as Traquair, and pasturage in the lands between Gala and Leader, where, as we have already seen, the monks were in constant dispute with the herdsmen of Wedale. More lands were acquired following the King's grants, and in time Melrose Abbey owned estates as far apart as Northumberland and Galloway.

The monks were, therefore, landlords and farmers on a grand scale – businessmen who administered a carefully ordered system. The largest proportion of their workforce were the villeins, bondsmen little better than slaves who lived and worked on the large farms. Above them were the cottars, who paid a few shillings a year to the monks for a simple dwelling and a small acreage; in return they had to put in a certain amount of work for the monastery. Next on the ladder were the husbandmen, who rented around twenty-five acres each. The typical services they had to render in addition to their rent were as follows:

Four days' reaping in harvest, the husbandman with his wife and all their family; and a fifth day, the husbandman with two other men.

One day carting peats, and one cartload yearly to the abbey.

The service of a man and horse once a year; the horse's load to be three bolls of corn, or two bolls of salt, or one and a half bolls of coals.

To till an acre and a half, and to give a day's harrowing with one horse yearly.

To find a man for the sheep washing, and one for the sheep shearing; these were to be fed from the monastery.

To serve with a wagon one day yearly, for carrying home the harvest.

The Cistercian order, of which the Melrose monks were the first representatives in Scotland, were devoted to frugality and to great strictness in their adherence to the monastic rule. They were, in theory, supposed to live by their own labours, and became early experts in agriculture. Their other main activity – the transcription of books and documents – has left posterity with one of the

The extensive foundations of Melrose Abbey give an idea of the scale of the medieval community there.

129

The grandeur of Melrose Abbey survives against the odds, desecrated by the ravages of time, war, and religious revolution.

earliest records of life in Scotland, the *Chronica de Mailros*.

The abbey itself gives us some idea of its one-time greatness, though invaders have burnt it, reformers hastened its decay, and later centuries compounded the vandalism of the past by using its remains as a quarry for new housing. Of the extensive convent buildings, only the foundations of the cloister remain, but the great abbey church, the still centre of so much activity and industry, stands partially roofed and relatively intact.

Melrose holds the heart of the greatest of Scotland's kings. As Robert the Bruce approached death from leprosy, his life's work in the establishment of his country's independence completed, he had one ambition left unfulfilled. He had wanted to lead a crusade, and he decreed that his heart was to be excised from his corpse after his death and carried on a crusade to the Holy Land. When I was a child every Scottish youngster knew the story of how the good Sir James Douglas carried that heart overseas and how, trapped by an ambush of Saracens, with no hope of escape, he hurled the casket containing the heart before him into the battle with the words, 'Lead on, brave heart, as thou wert wont to do; and I will follow.' Douglas died in that ambush, but the casket was retrieved and eventually interred at Melrose.

This story seems to indicate that Melrose Abbey was a particular favourite with Bruce: certainly he was responsible for its extensive rebuilding. But that work in its turn was demolished by subsequent invaders, and the ruins that we see today are a harmonious medley of the work of several centuries. The abbey church's most notable features are the flying buttresses, unique in Scotland, the magnificent tracery of the south transept window, the remnants of chancel vaulting and the decorated corbels.

Of all the architects and craftsmen employed in the creation and rebuilding of the Border abbeys, the name of only one is known to us – John Morrow, but he left nothing to chance: inscribed on the wall of Melrose's south transept are the following lines, roughly translated into modern English:

> John Morrow some time called was I
> And born in Paris certainly
> And had in keeping all mason work
> Of St Andrews the High Kirk,
> Of Glasgow, Melrose and Paisley,
> Of Nithsdale and of Galloway.

Scott's description of the ruins at night are some of the finest he ever wrote:

> If thou would'st view fair Melrose aright,
> Go visit it by the pale moonlight;
> For the gay beams of lightsome day
> Gild, but to flout, the ruins grey . . .

In no other area of Scotland is rugby followed with such enthusiasm as in the Borders. Here, a player makes an adventurous move during the Melrose 'sevens'.

The abbey is the setting every June for the picturesque crowning of the Melrose Festival Queen. Alongside are the peaceful National Trust gardens of Priorwood, and opposite is a recently established motor museum.

Modern Melrose is the home of the game of rugby sevens, and the Melrose rugby ground, the Greenyards, with its distinctive black and yellow goalposts, is the mecca for thousands of enthusiasts in mid-April. All the Border towns have their seven-a-side tournaments, either at the end of the main rugby season or at the beginning of the new one, but it was in Melrose that this variation of the game began, and it holds pride of place for 'sevens' throughout the world.

Amongst the villages around Melrose, Darnick has a fine example of an inhabited peel tower, and Newstead is the site of the ancient Roman fort of Trimontium. This quiet town and its surroundings were the scene of the greatest revolution this century in the treatment of Britain's mentally sick. In the 1940s Dr George Bell, superintendent of Dingleton Hospital, took the brave step of unlocking the wards. That this policy became accepted practice worldwide is in large degree due to the support and cooperation of the people of Melrose. The hospital is still renowned for its pioneering methods.

There are two visits to make on the road between Melrose and Galashiels. The first is to Abbotsford, that embodiment of Sir Walter Scott's vision of a feudal ideal, which began with simple intentions and ended as a baronial mansion. It is very much a shrine to his memory, run with great dedication and reverence by his descendants, Mrs Patricia Maxwell Scott and her sister Dame Jean. Here you can see his extensive library and his collection of mementoes of Border history and long-dead chivalry. And here too are some of the sad relics of his days of suffering, and evidence of his uniquely high standing among his contemporaries. During Scott's last illness, his bed was brought down to the dining-room at Abbotsford. His son-in-law and biographer, Lockhart, described the scene: 'It was a beautiful day – so warm, that every window was open – and so perfectly still, that the sound of all others most delicious to his ear, the gentle ripple of the Tweed over its pebbles, was distinctly audible as we knelt around the bed, and his eldest son kissed and closed his eyes.'

From the past, we come sharply into the twentieth century at the new village of Tweedbank and its industrial estate. It was created in the 1970s, proof positive of the government's intention to revitalize the Border economy by building the necessary housing and providing good space for factories. It got off to a promising start, and particular sensitivity was shown in the architecture and planning of the housing scheme, with old trees and hedgerows left intact. Encouraged by the incentive grants offered under the region's development area status, modest industrial units moved in. But the *laissez-faire* attitude of more recent governments has brought this development to a virtual standstill.

As we enter Galashiels from the south, it is only too obvious why the development at Tweedbank was treated with such aesthetic care by the government department concerned. Within view is the housing estate of Langlee, raping the countryside as surely as any invading army of the past.

FOURTEEN

INDUSTRIAL GALASHIELS

It may seem churlish to begin this chapter by continuing my description of the Easter Langlee housing scheme when Galashiels contains modern developments which have won several architectural awards. Nor are some of the other Border towns free of unsympathetic developments. But Easter Langlee is an eyesore which cannot be ignored, especially from the realigned A7 to the south. It is an example of the imposition by an outside body of architects of a standardized concept of building suitable for far more industrialized areas. It is utterly out of harmony with its site in the Border hills, and the plaque that adorns the road beside the scheme only emphasizes its incongruity. This tablet, commemorating Walter Scott's last journey home, marks where he 'Sprang up with a cry of delight' at the view that lay before him. If only the planners at Langlee had treated the pleasant parkland at their disposal with the same care they later showed at Tweedbank! If only the Galashiels Town Council had not compounded the folly by axing the avenue of fine old oaks by the roadside, whose preservation order proved to be an ineffectual defence! If only the contractors had done a better job ... Then perhaps there would not have been more complaints about this one scheme than about all the other housing projects in my constituency put together!

Galashiels' population is now only a few thousand less than that of Hawick, and its history is comparatively recent: until the Industrial Revolution it was a small village. But it shows signs of an ancient past. At Torwoodlee, home of the Pringle family, there is a Georgian mansion, and the remains of a peel tower. There are also traces of a broch, a mysterious conical-shaped Pictish stone building, so common in the Highlands and the Orkneys and Shetlands, so rare in the south of Scotland. Only the circular foundations of the Torwoodlee broch remain: its walls were carted away long ago for dyke-building. Perhaps a small contingent of Picts made their way here from the north for there are also the remnants of a substantial fort and terraces for cultivation, while from Torwoodlee to Peel Law there runs the unexplained 'Catrail', a trench and dyke from the Dark Ages which has long baffled archaeologists.

Galashiels appears in records as far back as 1124, when its name is given as 'Galche'. Variations on the theme included Galue, Galhe, Galwe and Galow, until in 1337 we find a closer approximation to its present form with 'Galashul'. The name probably derives from the words 'Gwala', meaning a full stream, and 'shiel', the Saxon word for shelter, found commonly throughout the Borders.

OPPOSITE *One of a pair of cowardly-looking lions guarding Glenmayne House, built in Victorian times for a wealthy Galashiels manufacturer.*

In early centuries, the settlement here was insignificant and primitive, a mere collection of huts. Even much later it retained a pastoral simplicity. This was captured by Robert Burns in the lovely poem celebrating the fine young men of Galashiels, which the town has adopted as its own; it was set to a traditional air arranged by Haydn:

> Braw, braw lads on Yarrow braes
>   Ye rove among the blooming heather;
> But Yarrow braes, nor Ettrick Shaws,
>   Can match the lads o' Gala Water,
>   Braw, braw lads.
>
> But there is ane, a secret ane,
>   Aboon them a' I lo'e him better;
> And I'll be his, and he'll be mine,
>   The bonnie lad o' Gala Water,
>   Braw, braw lads.
>
> Altho' his daddie was nae laird,
>   And tho' I hae meikle tocher,
> Yet rich in kindest, truest love,
>   We'll tend our flocks by Gala Water,
>   Braw, braw lads.
>
> It ne'er was wealth, it ne'er was wealth,
>   That coft contentment, peace or pleasure;
> The bands and bliss o' mutual love,
>   O that's the chiefest warld's treasure!
>   Braw, braw lads.

From the pre-industrial days described in the song dates Old Gala House, a modest and graceful mansion near the centre of today's town, and once surrounded by fine parkland. The original fifteenth-century tower on the spot carried this inscription:

> Elizabeth Dishington Builted me
> In sin lye not.
> The things thou canst not get
> Desyre not.

The house as we see it today – used as a centre by various local voluntary organizations – dates from 1583, though it has been considerably altered over the centuries. It is undoubtedly the most historically interesting building in Galashiels: originally the seat of the Lairds of Gala, it was vacated by them in the latter part of the nineteenth century as the surrounding parkland became urgently needed for the town's rapid industrial development.

The Victorian New Gala House of the Lairds of Gala achieved a strange fame in post-war years. During the Second World War it was used to house an evacuated girls' school from Edinburgh. Its name was St Trinians, and it was

Galashiels is the main shopping centre of the region, with a blend of traditional small shops and modern supermarkets.

made notorious by Ronald Searle who used it as the inspiration for his cartoons of truly terrible schoolgirls. As I write, this building is threatened with demolition, a victim of competing incompetence on the part of the now defunct town and county councils.

The Lairds of Gala, like those of Torwoodlee, were originally Pringles. The last male Pringle of the line died in 1650; his sister Jean had married Hugh Scott, a son of Wat o'Harden, and it is from this union that Christopher Scott, the present laird, descends.

The growth of Galashiels began with the Industrial Revolution. Since 1581 there had been an embryonic weaving industry here, as in most settlements with the raw product of wool close to hand. At this time there existed three 'Waulk Mills' – 'waulking' was the process by which the women treated the unfinished cloth by trampling on it steadily for hours at a time.

In 1666 the weavers first formed themselves into a corporate body, and in 1777 the Galashiels Manufacturers' Corporation, still an influential body over two centuries later, was formed. It bears the neat motto: 'We dye to live and live to die.' By this time the number of looms had grown to forty-three, and two hundred and forty women were working as spinners.

Fourteen years later an event occurred which placed Galashiels firmly on the road to industrial development and in the forefront of the woollen industry. George Mercer of Waukrigg Mill returned from a visit to Leeds with the knowledge, commitment and machinery to set up Scotland's first woollen factory of the new age. Galashiels became the centre of the Scottish tweed industry. (The name 'tweed' derives not from the river but from a mis-spelling of the word 'tweel' – twill – in an order from an English clerk.)

It was in the latter part of the nineteenth century that the real growth of Galashiels occurred, aided by the wars in Europe and America which helped to suppress potential competitors. The greatest leap forward came in the ten years following 1865, when the population trebled from five thousand to fifteen thousand. And if problems are caused by housing today, they pale beside those of a hundred years ago, when families crowded into houses darkened by the window tax, and with neither inside nor even outside lavatories.

Until the 1880s the boom continued. Workers made a reasonable living – indeed Galashiels wages were above the average – and the mill-owners themselves achieved considerable prosperity, as the substantial houses they built in the surrounding area testify. Industrial relations were harmonious, if feudal; the Gala manufacturers were sufficiently down to earth to be on Christian-name terms with their employees, sufficiently philanthropic to offer concrete benefits to the town, and far-sighted enough to put capital re-investment into improving the working conditions in the mills.

But the industry, always geared towards the export trade, was at the mercy of events beyond its control. In 1890 the United States Government imposed the McKinley tariff of just under fifty per cent on imported woollen cloth, and this figure was increased seven years later. The impact on Galashiels can be imagined. In a few years the workforce had dropped by a quarter, and there was mass emigration to America and the Commonwealth. From then on the industry's fortunes fluctuated, but never again reached its early peak. Increased trade with Europe improved things for a while at the beginning of this century, and then the First World War brought regular service contracts. It was not until 1920 that the next sharp decline occurred.

The home of the Scottish woollen textile industry : here, a weaver prepares a product for the export market.

This had a more radical cause than the imposition of tariffs. The high quality cloth of Galashiels was suitable for the made-to-measure tailoring that menswear in Britain had consisted of until then, but it was not geared to the mass production of cheap cloth for the new machine-made garments. Galashiels mills lost out to cheaper products from Yorkshire; and as developing nations began to produce their own textiles, they erected tariff barriers. Yet more emigration followed, this time mainly to New Zealand and Australia. The depression exacerbated the difficulties, and by 1937 five of the largest mills in the town were closed.

During the Second World War the situation remained unchanged, and although the post-war period was a time of expansion, it did not provide more jobs for the men of Galashiels. The dexterity required for work in the new mills was more suited to the nimbler fingers of women, and sadly there were no alternative jobs for the men to go to. The problem for the tweed industry now lay in attracting enough suitable skilled labour: at one point in the 1960s workers were being bussed in from as far afield as Dalkeith.

But the changes in fashion, and in particular the trend towards man-made fibre and denim cloth, have meant the inexorable decline of the woollen industry as it once was. In 1896 the mills of Gala boasted a hundred and twenty-eight carding sets and eleven hundred and twenty looms; in 1980 these figures were twenty and a hundred and two respectively. Increased technology, too, has played its part in this trend, and the mills that have survived have an impressive level of productivity.

With the decline of the woollen trade, the advent of a new, flourishing electronics and micro-circuits industry has brought salvation to the town. Abundant water, clean air and manual dexterity are three of the essentials needed for these concerns, and the natural resources of the region and the inherited skills of its workforce have these attributes in plenty.

It was the Gala Water that gave the town its original prosperity, making it possible to found the tweed industry here in the nineteenth century, for it was diverted into mill lades to provide free power. And in 1974, when the rest of British industry wound down to a three-day week, the owner of the Waverley Mill shook the dust off the old water-wheel, oiled its parts, and maintained full production. The wheel can still be seen in action in the museum which this enterprising mill now houses. But in the past in Galashiels, as in the other Border towns, the manufacturers of Victorian and Edwardian days paid scant respect to the waters to which they owed their living. Andrew Lang, writing his wonderful *Highways and Byways in the Borders* in 1912, never misses an opportunity to hammer home the degradation of the Tweed's tributaries. The Teviot at Hawick, the Ettrick at Selkirk, the Leithen Water, the Jed: at each town he raises his environmental standard. But Galashiels was a particular blackspot. Lang quotes the findings of an official report of 1906: 'It would be impossible to find a river more grossly polluted than the Gala as it passes through Galashiels', and he gives us his own description of it: 'The grey-blue liquid that sluggishly oozes down the river's bed among stones thick-coated with sewage fungus, is an outrage on nature most saddening to look upon. He does wisely who stands windward of the abomination.'

It is difficult to imagine all this now. Water purification and smoke control have cleared the river and the air at Gala; but there is no doubt that the council at the turn of the century was grossly negligent, and when its sense of priorities caused it to pursue the extending of the burgh buildings in preference to installing the much-needed sewage works, public opinion forced it to resign. At the ensuing election, only two of those who resigned were returned, and Galashiels got its sewage works.

I find Galashiels one of the warmest and friendliest of the towns, welcoming to any strangers in its midst. No group of incomers have been more aware of this than the colony of Poles and Ukrainians who settled in the town after the war had displaced them. Though the Polish club exists to remind them of their roots, so much are they a part of their new surroundings that the Braw Lad and Braw Lass, principals of the annual Braw Lads' Gathering around the end of June, have sometimes been known to bear Polish surnames rather than old Galashiels ones!

Leaving the town, we turn left immediately before a fine statue of the Border Reiver by Thomas Clapperton. He was a native of the town, and this is perhaps his best-known work. A little way along the main road is a group of well-built cottages and a larger building topped by a clock tower. These are the Lucy Sanderson homes, the earliest sheltered housing in Scotland. Built in the 1930s, they were the bequest of a member of the great manufacturing family of Sanderson. As well as the semi-detached cottages, there is a particularly fine communal hall with striking murals depicting the history of the town. Alas, it is little seen, as the hall is used only twice a week as a lunch club, and a trust deed severely restricts its use.

A left hand turn past the cottages brings us down to the Scottish College of Textiles, to which students from all over the world come to learn the skills of the industry. Beside it is the great Netherdale Rugby Football ground, where the town's club – one of the giants in the rugby world – plays host to visiting teams. (But I cannot pass it without remembering a day in 1970 that was in many ways the most difficult day of my political life, when I stood in protest outside the crowded ground on the last official tour by a South African side.)

Where Gala meets the Tweed a new bridge now towers over the water, and a quiet slip road follows the path of the river, giving a fine view across it to the grey walls and serried chimneys of Abbotsford. We lived along this road for two years, in the old Ferryman's house on the Gala estate, at the historic little settlement of Boleside. At that time there was still a station, and a small steam train still ran between Selkirk and Galashiels. In the autumn the train driver would stop a few hundred yards from Boleside station, climb on the engine cab, and pick crab apples from a tree that overhung the line.

A ferry, operated by a pulley system, used to cross the river between Boleside

The days of the border raids are recalled by this impressive statue of a reiver, which forms part of the Galashiels war memorial.

and Faldonside, ancestral home of the Kerr whose dagger struck the first blow in the murder of David Rizzio at Holyrood. In 1723 a boat carrying passengers to Melrose Fair capsized, with the loss of all on board. Legend quickly grew up that it was not the unsuitability of the craft, nor the fierceness of the current, which had caused the tragedy, but the intervention of the devil.

A more recent tragedy took place on this part of the Tweed in 1963, the year before I came to the Borders. In the Braw Lads Gathering the mounted procession led by the Braw Lad and the Braw Lass crosses the Tweed at Galafoot, and at Boleside on its return. It is a fine sight, the widest and deepest river crossing made during any of the Border festivals. Occasionally there are spills: in 1963 the young Selkirk standard-bearer was drowned at the crossing.

We rejoin the main road at the confluence of the Tweed and the fast-running Ettrick. Here it gushes down, brown foam swirling, to meet the pale and tranquil waters of the Tweed. At the ancient church of Lindean the body of Sir William Douglas, Knight of Liddesdale, Flower of Chivalry, murderer of Alexander Ramsey, lay for a night after his own murder in 1353. Victims of the Black Death were buried here, and superstition later saved the churchyard from desecration: there was a belief that, should the soil be disturbed, pestilence would again break out, as John Leyden's poem describes:

> Mark, in yon vale, a solitary stone,
> Shunned by the swain, with loathsome weeds o'er grown!
> The Yellow stonecrop shoots from every pore,
> With scaly sapless lichens crusted o'er:
> Beneath the base, where starving hemlocks creep,
> The yellow pestilence is buried deep.

143

FIFTEEN

THE SOUTERS OF SELKIRK

I once read that Selkirk is 'the proudest of all the Border burghs'. Whether this was an approving or a derogatory statement I am not sure. It is true that Selkirk is the most conscious of its past, the most insistent on its status as a royal burgh. Certainly it has many claims to fame, and associations with many great figures. The number of statues and tablets around the town centre testify to this. In the triangular market place stands Sir Walter Scott: the small courtroom where he administered justice for over thirty years lies just behind him. In front is the Pantwell, combining the old town cross with a drinking fountain which must have been a great focus for the exchange of news and gossip in the days when it supplied the town's water.

Just off the square are the old streets of Kirk Wynd and Back Row. By the 1960s the houses here had deteriorated badly, and a rebuilding programme was instituted. Care was taken to retain the historic layout of the streets, and a successful modern interpretation of the old centre won praise and awards for the town council. A final touch from the architect of the scheme shows how committed he was to its success in the eyes of the local people: a stone bas-relief on one of the walls depicts a figure working at a pair of boots, and it bears a remarkable resemblance to the last shoemaker in Selkirk. For Selkirk, though it had its other trades, was above all a shoe manufacturing town, and natives of the town are called souters (shoemakers), a name they carry with the utmost pride.

As the old Selkirk song puts it:

> It's up wi' the Souters o' Selkirk,
>   And down with the Earl of Home;
> And here's to a' the braw laddies
>   That wear the single soled shoon;
> It's up wi' the Souters o' Selkirk
>   For they are baith trusty and leal,
> It's up wi' the lads o' the Forest
>   And doon wi' the Merse to the deil –

In 1745, at the time of the second Jacobite rebellion, the souters of Selkirk received their most memorable order: they supplied boots for Bonnie Prince Charlie's army. But footwear was about all that this ill-fated expedition received from Selkirk, or from any of the Border towns: as he passed through

OPPOSITE *Golden larches backed by silver birches: a hillside in autumn, near Selkirk.*

145

them, he attracted very few recruits to his cause. There was no hostility, just disinterest. The Border counties had had their fill of warfare in previous centuries.

But an earlier and greater Scottish general had aroused a response here. At the ruined church in Kirk Wynd, a tablet commemorates the occasion in 1297 when the great William Wallace was declared Guardian of Scotland, and raised a company of archers from the men of Ettrick Forest. (The churchyard here holds the graves of the ancestors of Franklin Roosevelt.)

At the West Port plaques mark the places where Montrose spent his last night before the devastating battle of Philiphaugh, and also where Robert Burns stayed – and took a dislike to the town.

Making our way along the main street, we encounter a bust and a plaque commemorating the fine Scottish artist Tom Scott, whose birthplace this was. Andrew Lang, poet, scholar, writer and historian who lived from 1844 to 1912, was born at Viewfield, now the cottage hospital. The Langs were an old Selkirk family, and like Scott, Hogg and Buchan, Andrew Lang grew up on a diet of the great tales and legends of his native countryside. He contributed to this heritage when he wrote a series of wonderful tales for children; they have a quality of magic which he drew from his own boyhood: 'It was worth while to be a boy then in the south of Scotland, and to fish the waters haunted by old legends, musical with old songs ... One seemed forsaken in an enchanted world; one might see two white fairy deer flit by, bringing us, as to Thomas the Rhymer, the tidings that we must to fairy land.' The diversity and abundance of Lang's written work is amazing but it is probably for his children's books – *The Red Fairy Book, The Yellow Fairy Book, The True Story Book, The Animal Story Book* and so on that he is best remembered, and for his translations of Homer, on which I was reared at school.

Near Viewfield is the statue of the pioneering African explorer Mungo Park, who was born in Yarrow, a few miles from the town, and was apprenticed as surgeon there before embarking on his travels. Park went first to Sumatra: it was the experience that he gained there that led him to volunteer, and be accepted by the Africa Association, as the successor to a Major Houghton who had lost his life while trying to trace the course of the Niger. In 1795 Park sailed to the Gambia, where he disappeared into the bush for eighteen months. He was given up for dead, but reappeared to tell a tale of hardship, adventure and courage, and of the successful accomplishment of his mission.

He returned to the Borders to practise medicine in Peebles, but the lure of the unknown was too great to be ignored, and in 1805 he set off again for the West Coast of Africa. The expedition was doomed from the start. It was the rainy season; disease set in, and members of the party died from dysentery and fever. The survivors were subject to attack by animals and natives alike. By the end, less than ten of the original party of eighty remained. As they made their way by canoe through a rocky gorge near the village of Boussa, 'The people began to attack, throwing lances, pikes, arrows and stones. Mr Park defended himself for

Selkirk has several statues to her more famous sons, but this charming bas-relief of a souter depicts the shoe-making trade for which the town was famous.

a long time; two of his slaves at the stern of the canoe were killed; they threw everything they had in the canoe into the river, and kept firing; but being overpowered by numbers and fatigue, and no probability of escaping, Mr Park took hold of one of the white men and jumped into the water, and was drowned in the stream attempting to escape.'

The statue to Mungo Park's memory includes fine relief panels in bronze by Thomas Clapperton, who also sculpted the nearby figure symbolizing the event with which the traditions of the town are so inextricably linked: it bears the simple inscription, 'O Flodden Field'.

When James IV set out on his ill-conceived expedition against his brother-in-law Henry VIII in 1513, the men of Selkirk and Ettrick Forest rallied to his call. Selkirk was a favourite royal town; the yeomen of the forest received their lands not from a feudal baron but directly from the King, and to him they owed their military service. In the battlefield they formed the immediate defence force around their King, but their skill with their bows saved neither him nor themselves. (The skill itself survives, however: the Queen's Bodyguard of Archers in Scotland, an aristocratic company which attends royal occasions today, meets here every seven years to compete for the Selkirk Silver Arrow, the oldest archery trophy there is.)

According to legend, of the company of eighty able-bodied men who set forth from Selkirk to Flodden, only one returned, bearing with him a captured English flag. The flag can be seen in the excellent new museum at Halliwell's House in the market square: the tradition is enshrined in the pageantry of Selkirk's Common Riding.

Of all the Border Common Ridings, Selkirk, with over four and a half centuries of unbroken tradition, takes pride of place as the oldest, the largest and the most emotional. Let us follow the standard-bearer on what will probably be the greatest day of his life.

147

In the foreground of this panorama of the terraced streets of Selkirk are the mills which brought industrial expansion to the town in the nineteenth century.

Common Riding day in Selkirk takes place on the Friday following the second Monday in June (until the early seventeenth century it was in August, but little else has changed). The identity of the current year's standard-bearer is announced at the 'Picking Night' about five weeks earlier. He will be in his twenties, unmarried, and he must have ridden the marches behind previous standard-bearers at least four times, on two of which occasions he will have acted as an official attendant, sharing the duties and serving a kind of apprenticeship. But most standard-bearers far exceed the minimum requirements. (The 1984 holder of the office, Keith Monks, a young joiner, had an unbroken record of riding the marches since the age of ten; moreover his father was standard-bearer before him, and his young brother rides behind him.) He must have a reasonably unblemished reputation, and will be expected to have made a contribution to the life of the town. During the weeks leading up to the Common Riding, there are many and varied duties for him to perform, including the representation of Selkirk at other towns' festivities.

148

At four o'clock on the morning of the great day, the flute band wakes the provost and proceeds on a tour of the town, playing traditional airs and followed by an ever-increasing crowd of pedestrians. Just before seven a.m. they reach their destination, outside the Victoria Hall. The official party appears on the balcony, where the burgh flag, representing the one captured at Flodden, is tied with ribbons in the colour bussing ceremony. It is then entrusted to the standard-bearer, who is adjured to carry it round the marches and return it 'unsullied and untarnished'. He mounts his horse, the drum sounds, and the procession moves off along the main street, through the market place, and down the Green. Ahead of him, the silver band leads on, while the town's other banners are borne on foot behind him: those belonging to the historic trade guilds such as the weavers, hammermen (builders and joiners) and butchers; the flag of the merchant company, representing the shopkeepers; the British Legion's Union Jack heading a group of ex-servicemen; and the flag of the anachronistically named Colonial Society, the 'exiles' from Selkirk who have made their homes in the dominions of the Commonwealth, or even in the United States of America! The society's motto is 'Yince a souter, aye a souter', and every year sees a healthy contingent of those who take literally the words of the Common Riding song,

> Souters aye return to Selkirk
> When the roses bloom again.

Behind the representatives of the official bodies come hundreds of townspeople: groups of friends and families, parents with small children hoisted on their shoulders, old men with memories of Common Ridings long ago, and young boys who dream of the day when they too may ride in the standard-bearer's place.

The pipe band which follows them breaks the mood from revelry to solemnity, and behind it the lone standard-bearer leads the horsemen through the town to the River Ettrick. On this one day in his life he is set apart from other men, the central figure in this historic tradition.

At the riverside the foot procession disperses, leaving the riders on their own. On the far bank spectators in Linglie Glen can hear the cheers as the horses ford the river. At full gallop, six hundred stream up the narrow glen to the hills. The route they take, covering the boundaries of the burgh lands, is a hard one that traverses peaty bogs and dips and climbs over steep heather-covered hillsides strewn with hidden boulders.

There are only two stops on the twelve-mile journey. The first is at Tibbie Tamson's grave – in repentance, perhaps, for the cruelty and narrow-mindedness of some of Selkirk's eighteenth-century forebears. Tibbie was a simple-minded woman, an outcast much persecuted by her neighbours, who was accused of the theft of some yarn, and so much pressure was brought to bear on her that she hanged herself. As a suicide, her body was denied burial on consecrated ground, and even in death she was subjected to indignities by the

Selkirk Common Riding, 1984. LEFT AND OPPOSITE *The pipe band leads the procession through streets filled with onlookers and hung with flags.*

RIGHT *Riders ford the Ettrick before their inspection of the old burgh marches.* ABOVE *Standard-bearer Keith Monks casts the colours in the final ceremony of the Common Riding.*

people who had made her life such a misery. Her simple coffin was pelted with stones, and the body dragged out to the town's extremity, where it was buried by a countryman who showed greater Christian charity than Tibbie's neighbours. Today, on Common Riding morning, the grave always carries an anonymous tribute of flowers.

The second break takes place at the spot where three boulders, 'the three brethren', mark the contiguity of the burgh lands with those of two neighbouring estates. Here the riders dismount, the hip flasks are passed round, and after a chorus of the Common Riding song the standard-bearer leads the way over the hills, down beside Netley wood, to the return fording of the Ettrick and the gallop into town.

Back in Selkirk, all those on foot – standard-bearers and their followers, bands and townsfolk – remuster and march down from the town to the old toll. There they line the sides of the road and throng the banks while all eyes strain towards the distant horizon, where the returning band of riders will first appear. At last, on the faraway hill, a seemingly endless stream of horsemen wends its way down beside the wood on the other side of the Ettrick, and disappears again from view. Finally, to a crescendo of cheers, the Royal Burgh Standard-Bearer gallops alone, banner streaming, up the road into town. Hundreds of hooves thunder behind him, and the reverberating cheers of the crowd grip the riders in a spell of excitement. As the last horsemen straggle in, the focus of attention turns to the market place, where the final and most poignant of the morning's ceremonies is enacted: the casting of the colours.

It is this tradition that commemorates Flodden. The legend goes that Selkirk's lone survivor of that carnage, Fletcher, was too overcome to put his news of the disaster into words. Instead, in symbolism of what he had witnessed, he lowered the flag to the ground. This incident is re-lived every year in the casting of the colours, in which the banners of the town are waved in a series of prescribed patterns to the music of 'Up wi' the Souters o' Selkirk'. This ritual has no parallel that I know of in Britain, though there are flag-waving ceremonies in Italy and Belgium, and the custom may have common roots with other European traditions. The casting of the colours is a deeply emotional occasion, and many of the eyes that watch it are cloudy with tears. After the last flag is cast, that most haunting of all laments binds the crowd in a silence broken only by the ring of a restless hoof, the clinking of a bit or the voice of a child. 'The Lilting' is played at battlefields and remembrance ceremonies all over the world; but its inspiration was the desolation suffered in the small town of Selkirk four and a half centuries ago at the battle of Flodden Field, the most shattering and unnecessary of all Scotland's military disasters.

> I've heard them lilting at the ewe-milking,
> Lasses a' lilting, before the dawn of day:
> Now there's a moaning on ilka green loaning:
> The flowers of the Forest are a' wede awae.

At bughts, in the morning, nae blythe lads are scorning;
    Lasses are lonely, and dowie, and wae;
Nae daffing, nae gabbing, but sighing and sabbing;
    Ilk ane lifts her leglin, and hies her awae.

In Harst, at the shearing, nae youths are now jeering;
    Bandsters are runkled, and lyart or grey;
At fair, or at preaching, nae wooing, nae fleeching;
    The flowers of the Forest are a' wede awae.

We'll hear nae mair lilting, at the ewe-milking:
    Women and bairns are heartless and wae:
Sighing and moaning on ilka green loaning,
    The flowers of the Forest are a' wede awae.

As the proceedings draw to a close, the crowds give three cheers for 'The Royal Burgh Standard Bearer', 'Our worthy Provost' and 'Her Majesty the Queen', before drifting away for more private celebrations.

From Selkirk it is only six or seven miles to my home village of Ettrick Bridge, but instead of taking the direct route, I will go past my usual turn-off out of Selkirk and continue down the hill towards Yarrow before completing the circle. The road goes over the new concrete and steel bridge spanning the Ettrick, built in 1977 to replace the old stone bridge which was swept away in an unusually high flood. Turning left into Yarrow, Philiphaugh estate is on the right hand side. It was the scene of the last defeat of Charles I's cause in Scotland, and of the downfall of the colourful Marquis of Montrose, so beloved of historical novelists.

In the Civil Wars Montrose was originally on the side of the Covenanters, but by 1640 he had 'fallen in dislyke with [their] actings, and was now waiting for the first opportunity to cross them'. He crossed, indeed, into the King's party, and led a brilliant campaign on his behalf. The Highlanders, mainly Roman Catholic and excitable by temperament, rallied to him in the north, where he achieved a string of military successes. But as he proceeded south, the Highland soldiers drifted home, and he failed to capture the support of the Borderers. Nor did the latter flock in any numbers to the opposing standard of General Leslie. As in the next century, when Bonnie Prince Charlie took his route south, they simply opted out of the religious conflict.

Still, it was in this quiet valley in the heart of the Borders that the final drama was played out in 1645. The Royalist army had encamped at Philiphaugh, and its commander had taken up residence in Selkirk for the night. Despite rumours of Leslie's presence in the area, intelligence reports failed to locate him; all bedded down for a quiet night. But Leslie, heading northwards, was in fact at Melrose, and when he heard of Montrose's proximity, he seized the initiative. He marched towards Selkirk and, dividing his army, surrounded the sleeping troops. The Marquis, in his Selkirk lodgings, was brought the news of his

153

approach, instantly leapt on his horse, and, dishevelled and half-dressed, galloped down the hill and over the Ettrick towards the camp.

The battle was a sweeping victory for the Covenanters. Montrose and a few followers fled over Minchmoor to Traquair, and to the shadow of the scaffold in London. The prisoners taken at Philiphaugh were butchered with extraordinary savagery. Many were executed in the grounds of Newark Castle, and others shot in Selkirk market place. So ended the last battle fought on Border soil, leaving in its wake the intriguing mystery of Montrose's vanished and still unrecovered treasure chest, abandoned on the flight from the battlefield.

A little further on in Yarrow stands the crumbling shell of the cottage where Mungo Park was born, while the mighty ruin of Newark Tower overlooks the meeting of Yarrow Water with the Ettrick. Newark was the most substantial of all the fortified towers of Ettrick Forest, the property of the powerful Douglas family and a popular lodging for the Stuart kings on their hunting expeditions.

It lies within the grounds of Bowhill estate, the favourite seat of the Duke of Buccleuch. At Bowhill House itself the history of that great family can be traced from the far-off day, a millennium ago, when the Scotts found their way from Galloway to Rankleburn, half-way up the Ettrick Valley. John Scott had boasted of his prowess at hunting: he was given an opportunity to prove it before King Kenneth III. In a difficult chase, an antlered buck outpaced all its pursuers save Scott, who caught it by the horns and brought it to the King.

OPPOSITE Not only is Bowhill House – home of the Duke and Duchess of Buccleuch – set in a perfect natural environment, but it also houses a treasure-trove of exquisite works of art.

And for the buck thou stoutly brought
   To us up that steep haugh,
The designation ever shall
   Be John Scott of Bucks cleuch.

Through the centuries they rose, by almost unparalleled loyalty to the crown, to be the foremost family and the largest landowners of all the Border clans. In

LEFT *Newark Castle, owned by the great Douglas family, was confiscated on account of their treachery to the crown, and granted instead to the loyal Scotts of Buccleuch.*
ABOVE *Oakwood Tower stands on a craggy promontory halfway between Ettrick Bridge and Selkirk.*

the seventeenth century, ennoblement followed the union of the crowns. The dukedom came when Anne, daughter of the second Earl, married the Duke of Monmouth, natural son of King Charles II. Among the many interesting exhibits at Bowhill is the collection of Monmouth memorabilia, from his coral teething ring to the shirt worn at his execution.

The house itself is gracious rather than grand, and though its furniture, tapestries and porcelain are all of magnificent quality, it is in particular for its unique art collection that Bowhill is famous. The portraits of the family are by Van Dyke, Reynolds and Gainsborough: whoever was the leading portrait painter of the day. The Italian room has paintings by Guardi and Canaletto, and displayed in a darkened room to protect them are miniatures from the fifteenth century onwards, reputed to be the finest collection of its kind in the world. Nor will you find elsewhere, outside a publicly owned gallery, a painting by Leonardo da Vinci.

The setting of Bowhill, among woodland that shows the careful planting for which the estate is renowned, and with grounds sweeping southwards to the valley where the Ettrick runs, adds greatly to the attractions of this magnificent treasure-house.

Below Bowhill is the farm of Carterhaugh, the site each September for the annual show of the Yarrow and Ettrick Pastoral Society. Carterhaugh has an ancient magic, for it is the setting for what is often regarded as the most perfect of all the supernatural ballads. In 'Tamlane', Janet, a daughter of the house of March, defies advice to keep away from the woods of Carterhaugh:

> Oh I forbid ye, maidens a'
>   That wear gowd on yer hair
> To come or gae by Carterhaugh
>   For young Tamlane is there.
>
> There's nane that goes by Carterhaugh
>   But maun leave him a wad,
> Either gowd rings or green mantles
>   Or else their maidenhead.

The supernatural imagery, so strong in many of the ballads, is at its most powerful in 'Tamlane', though here, unusually, the unearthly forces are overcome by human fortitude.

The road by Carterhaugh brings us back to the Ettrick valley three miles from the village. Up to the left, in a commanding position, stands Oakwood Tower which looks across to its neighbour, Kirkhope. It, too, was one of the peel towers of the Scotts of Harden, and remains in a good state of repair, though uninhabited. Soon Kirkhope itself comes into view, and the houses of the village. We cross the bridge, with its stone taken from Auld Wat's bridge, and so return to the starting point of this journey round the Borders, whose countryside, history, legends and people I have come to know and love so well.

INDEX

Page numbers in *italics* refer to captions to illustrations